Discipline and Classroom Management

Third Edition

D. Keith Osborn
Janie D. Osborn

Education Associates
A division of The Daye Press, Inc.

Acknowledgements

We gratefully acknowledge the many persons who have made this publication possible. Among them are the professors who taught us, the college students we have worked with, our own children and our parents. But, most of all, the ones who really made this possible — are the children who allowed us to learn from them in the many years we taught in the classroom.

We lovingly dedicate this book to our daughter, Michelle.

Send mail orders to:
Education Associates.. Box 8021 .. Athens, GA 30603

© 1989 by Daye Press, Inc.

Printed in the United States of America
10 9 8 7 6 5 4 3 2 1

Library of Congress Cataloging-in-Publication Data

Osborn, D. Keith.
   Discipline and classroom management/ D. Keith Osborn, Janie
     Dyson Osborn, — 3rd ed.
     Bibliography:
     Includes index.
     1. Classroom management. 2. School children-Discipline
I. Osborn, Janie Dyson. II. Title
LB3013.074 1989   371.1'024—dc 19   89-1338
ISBN 0-918772-18-4 (cloth edition)
ISBN 0-918772-19-2 (pbk. edition)

Preface

As beginning teachers both authors remember that the most difficult task was not mastery of subject matter content ... rather it was learning how to deal effectively with children. There were situations when our best lesson plans were lost or wasted because of poor classroom management and control techniques. At times, an unruly kindergartner or a second grader can cause even the most competent teacher to question the wisdom of entering the teaching profession.

We should state at the outset that we definitely believe in discipline ... we feel that if a teacher cares about a child she will provide guidance and discipline.

We should also state that we do not believe that discipline and classroom management are magic — and, therefore, subject to some simple formula or mystical spell — nor is discipline a genetically endowed trait. A perfect class with few discipline problems does not happen overnight. The student should be aware that discipline is a slow process and hard to come by. It demands constant supervision and a teacher who is "with-it." When you find a situation of this nature, take a closer look and you will find many techniques being implemented in the "hidden structure" of the class

We believe that effective discipline and classroom management techniques are learned; therefore, a teacher can master the necessary skills. Chapter seven discusses sixteen major factors which are necessary for effective discipline. Learning to approach discipline problems with these factors in mind will help resolve many problems which arise in the classroom milieu. However, this text is not a cure-all ... there will always be times when it will rain four days in a row and Mondays will always come after holidays!

Good luck,

Keith and Janie Osborn

Introduction

Since 1969, Phi Delta Kappa has had the Gallup organization conduct a poll of the Public's Attitudes toward the Public Schools. By 1988, 17 of the 20 polls had rated school discipline as the number one educational concern. In the three polls in which discipline was not rated number one, it was viewed as the second most serious problem. Interestingly, while discipline has been a major concern throughout all these years, the types of discipline and child behavior problems have changed. To illustrate these changes, we offer the following statistics from the Police Department in Fullerton, California. In 1940 the top seven problems in the Fullerton public schools were: Talking, chewing gum, smoking, making noise, running in the halls, getting out of line, and wearing improper clothing. Contrast this with the top seven school problems today: Drug and alcohol abuse, pregnancy, rape, suicide, robbery, assault, and arson. Also high on to-day's list of school problems are absenteeism, extortion, vandalism, and gang warfare.

This is the third edition of our text on discipline and classroom management. We have used this text to supplement our beginning courses in education as well as a supplementary text in practicums where students are actually working with children. In our supervision with student teachers we have found the concepts discussed in the text are quite valuable in helping individuals gain useful classroom management techniques. After reading the text, the teacher can begin to diagnose her own approach to discipline and classroom management and see the consequences when she is inconsistent, lacks clarity, becomes stimulus bound, or engages in "over-kill" or "flip flops." Through studying the text the teacher will begin to consider her approach to the "target child" in terms of "audience children."

There are a number of theoretical approaches to discipline. Frankly, some of them have little practical value for the classroom teacher. We have avoided magic techniques, instant solutions and "buz" words which come and go — and, in the final analysis, do nothing to help the teacher in her day-to-day work with children. Every attempt has been made to present solid research results in meaningful, understandable terms which can be transferred to the classroom.

While the text utilizes four theoretical models — psychodynamic, behavior modification, social learning, and field theory — discussions of these frames of reference are kept to a minimum. Our aim has been to help students in practical ways to work with children rather than to pontificate theoretical structures. Basically the psychodynamic view examines antecedent conditions with respect to deviate behavior while other models are "ahistorical" being primarily concerned with the individual "in the present."

Chapter One and part of Chapter Two reflect the influence of the psychodynamic model. These chapters discuss the causality of behavior and ask the teacher to examine causative factors. Chapter Two particularly emphasizes the importance of the "emotional climate" in terms of the child's perception and acceptance of discipline.

Chapter Three discusses how children learn and reflects the behavior learning model. It shows how deviant behavior is learned and how new learning can occur with the subsequent modification of behavior. This chapter also discusses social learning theory and makes some generalizations concerning the modeling of behavior.

Chapters Four and Seven draw from field theory and demonstrate the utilization of this theory in the actual classroom. This model draws from Lewin's postulate that behavior is equal to a function of the person in the environment. Kounin's research particularly shows the influence of Lewin's theory and shows the impact individual behavior on the total classroom.

In Chapter Four we also examine the recent research on CBM; e.g., cognitive behavior monitoring, learning styles, and teacher effectiveness. Here again, we have attempted to select only those studies which seem particularly germane to the classroom teacher. One study by Emmer, Evertson, and Anderson (1980), will be of particular interest to teachers. The findings illustrating the importance of setting the stage in the classroom. These researchers found a significant relationship between effective classroom organization during the early weeks of school and effective discipline throughout the remainder of the year.

In the 1988 Gallup Poll mentioned earlier, the number one problem was drug abuse. Because of this rising concern we have enlarged our chapter on drugs. Chapter Five provides pertinent information on substance abuse. Our work with teachers has made us realize that often they know little of drugs or the drug culture. However, drugs have become so pervasive that they are affecting the school and the classroom. Chapter Five provides the teacher with pertinent information about the various types of drugs, the incidence of drug abuse, and many concrete suggestions which the parent, teacher and school can implement. Since drugs are beginning to filter down into the elementary grades, we have emphasized the importance of prevention. A special resource bibliography is also included at the end of Chapter Five.

With mainstreaming, we felt it would be helpful to include a chapter oriented to management techniques and the exceptional child. The authors wish to gratefully acknowledge the help of Virginia A. Boyle, Ph.D. Before entering private practice as a clinical psychologist, Dr. Boyle was an Assistant Professor in Special Education at North Georgia College. In addition, she has served as Director of the Community Developmental Center for Children and Chief Psychologist at the Intense Learning Center in Brunswick, Georgia.

One final word. Whenever possible we have used the plural form for child and teacher. However, it is often more convenient to refer to an individual child or teacher to illustrate a point. In these instances, in order to ease reading of the text, we have referred to the teacher as "she" and to the child as "he."

Table of Contents

*Chapter Six is written by Virginia A. Boyle, Ph.D.

Chapter One

Will the Real Problem Child Please Stand Up?

During the discussion period following any lecture on discipline many questions are raised. Usually, at least one teacher will direct a question to the speaker similar to the following: "I have a boy in my class who is quite aggressive. He is eight years old ... " It is, of course, impossible for the lecturer to answer meaningfully this type of question without further knowledge of the particular situation. Certainly many factors are involved. For example: What does the teacher mean by aggression? Is the aggression expressed physically or verbally? What is the frequency of the aggression displayed? What behavioral acts lead to the aggression? We could ask many other questions in connection with the teacher's problem and still remain unable to provide an adequate answer.

In many instances, the teacher who originally made the inquiry holds the answer to her own question — and the solution to her own problem. However, she must be willing to conduct a search within herself and to utilize the resources at her command. Many answers to behavior problems lay fallow within the teacher's own experiences; in her sensitivity to particular situations and in her ability as an observer.

In helping the teacher seek answers for dealing with a particular child, we would like to propose a series of questions. In utilizing this approach, the teacher will usually determine the source of the problem. In many instances, the solution may be embodied within her answers to these questions.

Am I the Problem?

Generally speaking, the more you know about a person, the better you can understand them. While this statement is not a "scientific law," it is certainly a good rule. This maxim applies to the children you teach — and, of course, this rule applies to you too! How much do you know about yourself? You probably visit your dentist and physician regularly for a physical examination; but when was the last time you gave yourself a "Teacher Check-Up?"

In order to understand the child's feelings, the teacher must recognize her own. To be able to empathize with a child's feelings of anger, the teacher should be aware of her own feelings of hostility and the events which cause her to become angry. In order to understand and accept a child's feelings of anxiety; the teacher must be willing to recognize these same feelings within herself. The teacher should be cognizant of the fact that unresolved conflicts in her own life can filter into the teaching situation and have a definite impact on her pupils.

The purpose of this section is to help the reader engage in some self-analysis to determine *one* possible source of a potential problem. Often we find that some apparent "problem children" are, in reality, adults with a problem. Usually, if we can resolve the adult problem — the child problem will also take care of itself. After reading and studying this section, you may wish to refer to the assessment items in Appendix D.

1. Why am I teaching anyway?

This question is so basic that it should be answered by every person *prior* to entering the profession of teaching. What personal needs does teaching fulfill? Sometimes an individual becomes a teacher in order to dominate and control others. Some persons want to work with children because they are unable to relate to adults. Needless to say, these are not valid reasons for entering the teaching profession.

Some teachers tend to identify too greatly with their pupils. In doing so the teacher's ego becomes so highly involved that every pupil's success is a personal triumph. Every pupil failure becomes a personal failure and rebuff to the teacher. The net result is a "pressure cooker" classroom setting in which children suffer under high teacher demands and unreasonable expectations. In examining her philosophy the teacher should ask, "What is really significant; what really counts in my teaching?"

2. Is "what really counts" significant?

At times situations can arise and teachers become bogged down in minutiae. We once knew a teacher who wanted all the children to place their pencils on the desks with the erasers pointed in the same direction. We have known a few kindergarten teachers who were unhappy when the slightest paint was spilled. Some of these teachers felt they had "problem children." Instead, the children had compulsive, slightly neurotic teachers. Once, when conducting some research on discipline, we developed the category, "too much issue" to describe this type of adult. In our study we encountered parents and teachers who often made a big issue out of a small problem. In our observations we saw a father spank a three year old who let the screen door slam; we knew one second grade teacher who made children stay in during recess if they forgot to write their names on their paper. We observed a high school teacher give five hours of extra work because a boy left his seat to sharpen a pencil. While these matters can be disturbing, we felt that the adults were creating "too much issue."

3. What do children do that upsets me?

In many ways, this question is the most significant one in our checklist. Remember to consider things which cause minor upsets. Little problems, like small bills, can really add up. For example, some teachers become overly concerned with time. They become rigid in their adherence to a schedule. If a child falls behind ... the teacher becomes irritated and forgets her real purpose in teaching. Everyone has minor prejudices and these do effect the way we deal with people. Some teachers are overly concerned with manner of dress and may unconsciously punish children who do not dress well. Some adults are prejudiced against fatness, cuteness, ugliness and poor language patterns. In a number of cases, the child does not have the problem — rather, the teacher has a prejudice which she must learn to handle. Often, merely recognizing the problem makes it become more manageable.

4. Is my approach to children clouded by my own childhood experience?

It is impossible to keep your own childhood experiences from entering into your approach to children. Often these experiences can be helpful in our vicarious understanding of others. At times, however, they can interfere. As mentioned in the statement above, our own prejudices can effect the way we work with children.

Often parents want their children to succeed in areas where they failed as children. They push and pressure children to be popular, date sooner, read better or make first string in Little League football. The mature adult is capable of accepting other selves for what they are, rather than what the adult would like that person to be. A nervous, distraught child is often a normal child who has become upset and anxious as a result of misguided adult pressures. For example, in children over five years of age, chronic enuresis (bed wetting) often occurs when youngsters are under unusual stress or excess parental pressures. Guiding learning means working with children so they can discover, create, and develop to their fullest capacity.

5. Am I tired or upset?

One rainy Monday in my first year of teaching the morning was going particularly bad. The children seemed unusually noisy and argumentative and I was beginning to question the wisdom of my decision to enter the teaching profession. At that moment Mavis grabbed Cindy's book and I grabbed Mavis and said sternly, "No, No, No!!" Mavis shrugged her shoulders and said plaintively, "Teacher, do you realize you have been saying, 'No' all morning?"

When you think you have a problem, ask yourself, "Is this just one of those days?" You know — we all have "those days." Unless care is taken, the tired or worried teacher creates her own problem situations. Lack of sleep, concern over the illness of a loved one, unpaid bills, an unthinking principal, four days of rain — many factors can contribute to making the work situation difficult. During these periods — whenever the teacher is fatigued or worried — even minor problems can assume major proportion.

In summary

Be honest with yourself and in your approach to the questions raised in this chapter. Research has shown that there are times when teachers do operate under stress. Worrying about your own children, your husband, the school administration are all factors which impact on a teacher when she is in the classroom. Answering the items discussed in this section may provide insight into that so-called "problem child." In addition, you may wish to examine the assessment items in Appendix D. These items are designed to help you see if you are meeting your goals in terms of discipline.

Despite low pay and minor problems, teaching is a challenging rewarding profession. One of the most satisfying experiences is to watch children grow socially and intellectually. If relating to children in this way does not excite you and "turn you on" — we strongly suggest that you review your answer to the first question.

Determining the problem: A case study

When the teacher satisfies herself that she is *not* the problem, she should begin to gather information which will prove useful in diagnosing the child's trouble. When the teacher recognizes a student's needs it minimizes confusion about student failure or misbehavior. It suggests ways to handle behavior problems and enhance learning. There are three major considerations in studying individual behavior. One is an empirical question: "How does a person actually behave in a given situation?" The second issue is a theoretical one, "Why does he behave as he does?" The third is a practical question: "What can I do to help this child?"

While it is not the purpose of this treatise to discuss data collection in detail, this section will provide some guidelines which can help the teacher answer the initial question, "How does the child actually behave?" Prior to implementing any detailed plan of action the teacher should conduct a simple child study. Three essential ingredients are needed in preparing such a study: description, observation and interpretation.

1. A description of the child

The first part of a child study should concern itself with a general description of the child. The birthdate, sex, height, weight, overall physical condition and appearance should be included. If the child is taking medication, has any allergies or unusual physical maladies — these should be noted. There should be a short statement concerning the child's parents and siblings. If there are any unusual home circumstances (parents divorced; father not permitted to visit child; child lives with grandparent) these should be included in your general statement. In addition the teacher should provide a short summary describing the child physically, socially, emotionally and intellectually. Any unusual interests, abilities or attitudes in these areas should be mentioned. The purpose of the general description is to provide the reader with a "feel" for the youngster being observed.

2. Observation

The teacher should make a number of observations of the child. A good observation should present an accurate account of the child's behavior. A person reading the observation should be able to visualize the same picture as the person who observed the original event. The following suggestions will be helpful in gathering a complete and accurate record.

• Date each observation and indicate the time of day.

• Indicate the duration of an event or events:
  — How long did the child cry; listen to a record.
  — How long was the child involved in reading a book.

• Indicate persons and events which are reinforcing.
  — Best friends; favorite friends.
  — Preferred activities; favorite game.

• Include actual dialogue, where possible.
  — *Instead of:* T. told child to leave room and he refused.
  — *Report:* T. said, "Leave this room immediately and do not come back until you learn to behave." Gloria threw her book on the floor, stamped her foot and said, "I didn't do it and you can't make me leave!"

• Describe the situation in which the behavior took place.
  — In some instances it may be helpful to make a drawing of the room, the location of the children, the location of the equipment, the location of the teacher.

• Include full details of the activity.
  — *Instead of:* He played in the dramatic corner.
  — *Report:* Mike sat in the dramatic corner with three small rubber dolls. He placed the mother doll in the living room area and put the baby doll in the high chair. He took the father doll and said to me, "This is the papa; he is going to spank the baby for throwing food."

• Describe actions, rather than labelling.
  — Avoid the use of labels. For example: Fun-loving, spoiled brat, possessive, lazy, introverted. Rather report the actual behavior which has occurred.
  — *Instead of:* Brenda is highly dependent.
  — *Report:* Brenda will not leave my side during recess. If my hands are not engaged in actually holding some object, she will take my hand and not let go of it.

• Avoid pseudo-descriptive terms.
  — Some terms do not describe. However, they appear to be bona-fide descriptions, and give the reader a psychological "set" (prejudgement) concerning the child. Examples: He is always late ... she never does her homework ... she is highly possessive ... he is just naturally lazy ... he is very stubborn and always refuses to cooperate.

One method of observing would be to gather several short five to ten minute samples of each day over a period of one to two weeks. The time samples should be taken during different segments of the day in order to achieve a balanced picture of the child's behavior.

3. Interpretive comments

A case study should also contain the teacher's interpretive comments. However, these evaluative statements should be placed at the end of the report and labelled so the reader understands the statements are interpretive, rather than actual descriptions of behavior. Appendix C contains observations and an analysis for gathering data. For the student who wishes to study methods of observation and data collection in greater detail, consult the references in the bibliography.

Physical and psychosocial considerations

The preceding section addressed itself to the question: "How does the child actually behave in a given situation?" In many instances day-to-day observations of general behavior will provide the teacher with sufficient information to plan appropriate ways of working with the child. For example, daily observations may reveal that the teacher is using inappropriate reinforcement techniques — or that her techniques are inconsistent — or lack clarity. The study of Sam (Chapter Three) shows the value of observation in planning strategies for altering behavior. Observation #1 in Appendix C illustrates how observation can provide insight into problems which arise in the course of an ordinary school day.

However, if the difficulty still persists, we suggest the teacher carefully study the following questions which deal with rather specific physical and psychosocial considerations. The remainder of the chapter will provide some insight into why the child behaves as he does. The chapter will also present suggestions on what can be done when solutions are beyond the scope of the educator's training.

Except for the first item, the child's physical condition, the questions are not presented in any order of importance. The teacher should examine all the questions which are raised in this section and investigate all areas as an integral part of her overall evaluation.

1. Is the child physically sound?

Many so-called behavior problems hide behind poor health. We have known several good teachers who were looking for psychological symptoms and discovered poor vision, poor hearing or poor metabolism instead.

Once we were visiting a Head Start center in Boston and the teachers asked us to observe Frank, a four year old who was a "biter." The teachers also described Frank as "nervous" and "hyperactive." As we observed Frank that morning he bit two children and seemed to be constantly in motion.

Coincidental to our visit that day a dentist was at the center conducting preliminary dental examinations. At noon all of us had lunch together. Before any discussion of Frank occurred the dentist remarked to the head teacher, "I would like to schedule an appointment for Frank as soon as possible. The condition of his mouth and gums is terrible. He must be in constant pain." Then the dentist added casually, "Of course, I know you are surely aware of his poor physical condition — because the pain is obviously causing him to be highly active and nervous."

Two months later we saw Frank's teacher. She informed us that following substantial dental work Frank had "calmed down" and stopped biting.

A child who is mentally retarded can present problems which appear to have psychological origins. Since about thirty children in every 1,000 are diagnosed as mentally retarded, the teacher should be alerted to this possibility. A mentally deficient child will never catch up to the average child his age. As he grows older, he falls farther behind. However, Dittman points out (1988, p. 137): "Except in cases of extreme mental retardation, parents and teachers can help mentally retarded children develop. The way family and others treat a mentally retarded child has a lot to do with whether or not the child can remain emotionally healthy and well adjusted."

Often mental retardation is diagnosed during infancy — but many children are not identified until nursery, kindergarten, or public school. There have been instances where an alert teacher detected the problem after it had been overlooked by parents and medical personnel. (See Chapter Six for a discussion on the exceptional child.)

Some children experience illnesses which necessitate frequent absences from school. It is not unusual for the child to become passive or assume the stance of an "onlooker" since establishing and maintaining friendships is difficult with intermittent attendance. In some instances the child may become aggressive in order to gain attention from other children. With such cases the teacher may need to make special adjustments to ease the child's re-entry into the classroom and to help him feel he is a part of the group.

Various physiological deficiencies can also effect behavior. One of the biggest "problem creators" is lack of sleep. Too often parents allow children to stay up late and watch television. A recent survey by the National Association for Better Broadcasting found that seven million children (ages 2-11), watched television as late as 11 PM. When a child is tired and lacks sleep he becomes irritable and cranky. The medical profession now refers to this problem as, "TV-itis," since parents are bringing their youngsters to pediatricians and complaining of tired, listless cranky children.

Some children are taking medication or a combination of drugs as prescribed by the pediatrician or psychiatrist. At the beginning of the year determine which children are on

11

medication and the type of medication used. Individuals who are taking "common" drugs may display unusual and even bizarre symptoms. Ask the parent if there are any unusual symptoms (like drowsiness, slurry speech, irritability, poor coordination, dilated pupils) associated with ingestion of the drug. Presently one of the most commonly prescribed drugs for young children is Ritalin. All of the symptoms mentioned above can occur with youngsters who are taking Ritalin.

If this is your first year of teaching in a particular school system, determine the policy concerning dispensing drugs during school hours. School systems do vary in their procedures on drug intake. Some systems allow the teacher to dispense; others prefer that this task be delegated to the school nurse or principal. Most systems will not dispense any drugs without written permission from the parent or physician.

Unfortunately you may have a youngster who is taking an unauthorized or illegal drug. Drug abuse has become a problem of epidemic proportion in the United States and some children as early as eight to ten years of age are involved. A sad truth is that an initial drug encounter may occur on school grounds. Unusual changes in behavior — a drugged, sluggish appearance, unusual euphoria, slurred speech, a quiet demeanor, red eyes — may all be symptoms of drug use. Because of the rapid escalation in the drug problem, Chapter Five is devoted to this situation and specific suggestions are provided to the teacher.

Inadequate nutrition can also effect behavior. A teacher from Alabama related the following incident: "One summer I taught in a Head Start program. Each morning we served breakfast to the children because we knew that they were not receiving an adequate meal before coming to the center.

"That fall, when I returned to my public school position, most of the Head Start children were placed in my first grade class. However, I was shocked at the drastic difference in the behavior of these children.

"In the public school setting they seemed less active, sluggish and docile. I began to wonder if, somehow, the more formal school setting was inhibiting their behavior. As time passed, however, I began to notice a slight change. The children did begin to become more active and attentive — but, to my amazement, this behavior change occurred only in the afternoon!

"Several weeks later it struck me! The increase in activity was occurring immediately following the lunch hour! After consulting with the lunchroom manager, we made arrangements to provide the children with a breakfast snack when they arrived each morning. Within a short period of time a noticeable change in the children's behavior had taken place."

The American Nutrition Council reports that almost twenty percent of American children under six years of age consume less than the recommended daily intake of calories. In low income families almost one-third of the young children have insufficient caloric intake. Pre-teens and adolescents also have poor eating habits. Some teenagers attempt to survive on a diet of pizza, potato chips, and cola drinks. While the effects of moderate malnutrition are not completely understood, studies suggest that malnourished children tend to lag in behavioral development, motor skill performance, reading ability, concentration and motivation. It is almost impossible for the child to learn when his hunger needs are not satisfied. A hungry child is nervous, listless, poorly motivated and disruptive. Several states have begun to recognize this problem and have legislation requiring schools to provide both breakfast and lunch to students.

Some physical illnesses, like hypoglycemia, may carry symptoms which appear psychological and manifest themselves in peculiar behavior. A child with dyslexia may be placed under considerable pressure because the adult feels the child is not motivated to learn. Unless the teacher is fully aware of the physical problem she may mistakenly respond to the psychological symptoms and delay the necessary medical treatment. Recent nutritional research raises questions concerning some food colorings and food additives which also effect both growth and behavior. Our own daughter is highly allergic to red food dyes. If she ingests even a small quantity of these dyes, her behavior becomes hyper; e.g., she is very talkative and unusually physically active.

We strongly suggest to teachers that if they suspect a severe behavior problem they should initially consult the school nurse or physician to determine whether or not the problem has its etiology in a physical area.

2. What is the child's cultural background?

The term "culture" is used here in a broad sense and includes children representing various backgrounds and social situations. Problems can arise when children come from a home possessing values which are at variance with the teacher of the school system. It is important for teachers to recognize these cultural differences in order to correctly interpret and understand the child's behavior.

For example, most teachers typically want children to maintain eye contact during a conversation. When a youngster is being disciplined, teachers expect eye contact as a sign of attention and respect. However, in some cultures, children have been taught to avoid eye contact. In certain cultures, maintaining eye contact with an authority figure would be interpreted as an act of defiance.

In a study with day care families Elardo and Caldwell (1973) found that one of the important differences between teachers and parents was in the area of aggression. While the teachers discouraged fighting, parents felt their children should be aggressive and defend their rights. Caldwell (1977, p. 10) reports, "We have had parents pick their son up from school and then drive around the school campus looking for another child who supposedly had insulted their son — in order that, when the other boy was located the son could get out of the car and beat the boy up. Similarly, we had a child whose parents had 'dared' him to come home from school without having beaten up the little boy who threw sand in his sister's eyes while they were playing together the previous weekend."

In another situation a teacher acquaintance had asked her third grade students to write an essay entitled, "My friends, the Police." One child responded, "But, Ms. Bennett, the police ain't no friends of mine. They put my mother in jail."

A teacher from Michigan shared the following: Lauren was a kindergarten child who seemed unable to share. When playing in the doll corner, she would gather all the dolls to herself and not allow anyone else to touch them. If Lauren was at a table coloring, she would hoard all the crayons. The teacher made an interesting discovery during a home visit. The home was completely devoid of toys, play materials or other items which a young child would enjoy. Lauren had almost no previous experience with play materials and, consequently, wanted them "all to herself."

Recently, across the nation, we have had a dramatic increase in the number of foreign pupils. One of the most obvious problems is the language barrier. A number of children come to school who cannot speak English. Obviously, it is very difficult for youngsters to conform to the teacher's instructions if they do not comprehend basic English. Teachers cannot expect compliance from children who do not understand simple instructions or basic commands. Five year old Bonita came to kindergarten with her mother. Neither she nor the mother spoke any English. After some "sign language" the mother deposited Bonita and abruptly left. Bonita was hysterical. In spite of the teacher's attempts to comfort Bonita, the youngster continued to cry. Fortunately another teacher spoke fluent Spanish and was able to calm Bonita's fears that her mother had abandoned her with a strange person in a strange place.

Teachers should be aware of the religious backgrounds of their students since some religions place restrictions on the activities of their members. These restrictions may make children reticent to participate in some school activities. For example, some religions prohibit pledging allegiance to the flag, the celebration of any holidays, including birthdays or the viewing of motion pictures — even if educational in nature. Some religious organizations may accept movement education but prohibit dancing.

3. What is the child's learning ability?

A behavior problem may really be a learning problem. Research suggests that when a pupil's level of aspiration is incompatible (by being either too high or too low) with his performance ability, there is pressure to "leave the field" of learning. In our interviews with children we encountered youngsters who were "bored" with school. In a number of instances the child was capable of a high level of performance but teacher expectations were slight. As a result the child quickly finished his assignments and drifted into trouble.

Obviously the reverse holds true. Some children have a level of aspiration which far exceeds their performance ability. One fall we interviewed Ralph, an eleventh grader, who indicated his desire to become a medical doctor. His school grades were quite poor — mostly C's and D's. We asked him how he thought he could enter college with such poor grades. He replied that he was sure his grades would improve during his junior year. In the Spring we were conducting some follow-up interviews with the same children. We learned that Ralph had dropped out of school and was working in a car wash. Unfortunately no one at the school had been able to help Ralph determine a more realistic level of aspiration. As a result he simply "left the field" of learning. One of the tasks for the teacher is to help children realistically set goals which are attainable and help students develop strategies for reaching these goals.

Some children have physiological problems which make learning difficult. This child may appear to be disruptive in a deep psychological sense. Kephart (1971, p. 5) presents an enlightening description of this youngster: "To most teachers, as well as parents, the slow learning child is a complete enigma. One day he learns the classroom material to perfection; the next he seems to have forgotten every bit of it. In one activity he excels all other children; in the next he performs like a two year old. His behavior is unpredictable and almost violent in its intensity. He is happy to the point of euphoria but, the next moment, he is sad to the point of depression."

In the section, "Is the child physically sound," we mentioned dyslexia. Usually children with dyslexia are not mentally retarded. However, children diagnosed as dyslexic often encounter pressure under the erroneous idea that they are not motivated to learn. Some may become highly upset since they cannot read as well as their classmates. While physicians do not have a specific cure for dyslexia, qualified reading specialists can often help the child.

A word of warning: Often "slow learners" and "dyslexia" are used as "catch all" terms for any general problem or reading disability. The teacher should avoid the pitfall of labelling a problem since a label can provide "false comfort" and delay parents from conducting a search for some workable alternatives. In such situations the teacher should recognize her own limitations and be prepared to make a referral to professionals trained to work with specific problems beyond the scope of the average teacher. The reader is referred to Chapter Six. This chapter is specifically addressed to management techniques and the exceptional child.

In the meantime the teacher should learn to focus on the specific problem which is upsetting to the child. If she can isolate the specific trouble and systematically work to effect a solution — she may solve the problem or make definite headway toward its ultimate resolution.

4. Is this a case of school "cultural shock?"

Four out of five children move to a new residence every eighteen months. In many cases the child also moves to a new school. Teachers should recognize that a new home and a new school can represent "culture shock" for the child. Usually the move means learning new surroundings, making new friends and adjusting to a new teacher.

The following example is fairly typical: Ginger, age seven, had recently transferred to a new school. She resisted going to school and was having difficulty sleeping. Ginger merely said, "I don't like school any more!" After a lengthy investigation and consultation with the new teacher the real problem emerged. In the new school the teacher expected the children to use cursive handwriting. In Ginger's old school the children used manuscript; cursive handwriting was not taught until the third grade. Ginger did not understand cursive writing but was afraid to tell the teacher for fear of reprisal.

Culture shock can occur within the same system when a child moves from one grade to the next, as seen in the following example. Merritt had a third grade teacher who gave high grades and required little from her pupils. Merritt received all A's from this teacher. The following year she moved to a new school in another section of the city. Merritt's fourth grade teacher demanded a great deal from her pupils and had high grading standards. In reviewing third grade material the first few weeks, several things were apparent. Merritt was spending long hours preparing her homework; her test scores were B's and C's. Merritt became nervous and cried when it was time to go to school. Because of the difference in performance from the previous year, the teacher requested a conference with the parents. This conference revealed curriculum differences and the differences in grading between the schools and the teachers. Recognizing the problem the teacher became more empathetic and provided individualized work until Merritt was able to catch up with her classmates.

The move from elementary school to middle school can be traumatic for some children. This may be particularly true if fourth grade children are housed in a building which also has eighth grade youngsters. The differences in psychological development between a nine year olds and fourteen year olds are worlds apart. Reactions toward the peer group, teachers, parents, and other adults are dramatically different and these differences can be upsetting to the younger children.

5. Is the child reacting to some unknown situation in the home environment?

Parents can pressure their children and the result can manifest itself in the classroom. For example: Beth was an extremely bright five year old. An only child, her mother was an attorney; her father a psychologist. The parent's academic expectations for Beth were quite high. At two years of age she loved classical music, her parents taught her to read when she was four. In kindergarten her language facility was that of an adult. Late in the kindergarten year she was reading at the sixth grade level.

However, Beth did not like kindergarten. She was unable to get along with her classmates. She tried to boss them but they would not conform to her demands. She was unable to share with others and spent most of the class day in the corner reading a book. At group time she was inattentive or wanted to dominate a conversation. When not given her way, she would throw a temper trantrum — stamping her feet, screaming and crying. For the most part, Beth only worked well with the teacher and was unable to communicate with the children.

In a conference the teacher shared her problem with the parents. The parents agreed that Beth's behavior was such that she needed psychological help. Several months later, in the first grade, Beth began to improve. She had learned to share and was beginning to relate more meaningfully with other children.

One afternoon the father stopped by to see the kindergarten teacher. He happily related Beth's progress and then added, "We just expected too much of Beth academically. We spent too much time teaching her to read but never gave her the opportunity to socialize with others."

Divorce can create problems which affect the child's performance in school. Statistics reveal that one marriage in three ends in divorce — thus there are very few classrooms which are immune to this situation.

Studies on divorce indicate that children do suffer as a result. They may make high demands upon the teacher when the divorce is in progress. Our own observation is that psychologically the child may reach out to the teacher and demand more attention. An interpretation of this behavior might be that the child is seeking strength and reassurance in the one adult in his life who seemingly has remained stable and predictable — in this case that adult may be the teacher.

There is no such thing as a victimless divorce. One study on preschool children found that nearly 50% of the children involved in a divorce displayed significant psychological problems one year following the divorce. We have known a few uncontested divorces in which both parents were very cooperative and agreeable in the case of child custody. However, even in these cases situations arise where the adults have arguments and the child becomes concerned and upset. We have never seen a single case where a divorce has not had an impact on the child. In most cases the effect will be reflected at school.

Some school-aged children respond to divorce with extreme melancholy and sadness, fear, feelings of loss and deprivation. Studies suggest that during this traumatic period boys become highly aggressive and disturbed. Children may fear they are being rejected and displaced.

A divorce can create many changes and new problems. Father is absent from the home; father takes the child for a visit ... or, if father is awarded custody, then mother will see the child on a limited basis. If one of the parents moves from the city, then the child will face even more limited visitation from the parent who was not awarded custody. In some cases a new stepparent or a housemate may enter the home; in other situations the child may move in with the grandparents and see the parents on a limited or haphazard basis. If child abuse or drugs are involved in a divorce, one of the parents may be refused visitation rights.

Custody fights and financial hassles over alimony are extremely traumatic and can severely threaten children and affect their behavior. Skeen and McKenry (1980) have an excellent article on the role of the teacher in facilitating a child's adjustment to divorce. In their article they summarize many of the behavioral reactions which one may witness in children. They also provide an excellent bibliography for teacher and parent as well as appropriate books for pre-school and school aged children.

Child abuse is a problem which can certainly impact on the school. Teachers must be aware of the signs of child abuse and be ready to deal with such problems. Children who have been abused need understanding, warmth and acceptance from the adult world. In many instances, the youngster may need counseling and/or medical attention.

In most states, if a teacher suspects that abuse has taken place, she is required, by law, to report the abuse to the proper authorities. If you are not aware of the legal requirements for your state or community, you should consult with the principal to determine the proper reporting procedures. The teacher is advised to take notes and make a record of the events which led to the conclusion that abuse had occurred.

The teacher must be aware that children do not come to school in a vacuum. Mother's illness, Daddy's new job, a parent on drugs, a new baby sister all attend school in the mind of the child. The problems of the home do come to school.

6. Is the child reacting to some unknown situation in the school environment?

Problems can arise in school, but away from the pupil's classroom. In these instances the teacher may be totally unaware of the total Gestalt and its effect on the child. A strict, irritable bus driver and a bus load of rowdy, boisterous children is enough to make a quiet, shy first grader wish he did not have to go to school. Initially the three incidents which follow were quite mysterious:

Quite suddenly and for no apparent reason, Cheryl, aged four, did not like to attend nursery school on Thursdays. After some questioning, the teacher discovered that the Thursday car pool mother allowed the family cat to ride in the car. While the other children enjoyed this guest passenger, its presence was terrifying to Cheryl.

Winston, a third grader, had recently moved to a new school. After two weeks, Winston told his parents he wanted to move back to their old neighborhood. When he was asked why he was unhappy, Winston would become uncommunicative. The teacher could report nothing in the classroom which was contributing to this unhappiness. However, she had observed that every afternoon, during the final period, Winston would become nervous, upset, and highly active. A short time later, and quite by accident, the teacher discovered that every afternoon on the way home, Winston was being beaten by a group of fourth grade boys.

Virginia, a fifth grader, would not go to the bathroom. Investigation showed that some kids were smoking pot in the girl's restroom and this behavior upset Virginia. However, peer pressure made her afraid to tell the teacher.

7. What is the child's role with his peer group?

All teachers are aware of the influence children have on each other. Research studies (Lewis and St. John, 1974; Bailey and Kackley, 1975) show that the peer group can play an important role in influencing behavior and classroom learning. Teachers should be aware of any cliques, gangs, or other groups which may scapegoat or otherwise unduly influence other children. In some school settings there can be conflict between a minority group and the majority group. Peer pressures can be detrimental to student safety and learning.

In our camp one summer we had a nine year old, Teddy, whose behavior seemed incomprehensible. At breakfast Teddy would often take his cereal bowl, turn it over his head and allow its contents to dribble down his face. Whenever possible, the counselor would prevent this activity; however, if the transgression occurred, Teddy was immediately punished. It was also obvious that the boys did not think it funny, since the visual impression of the incident usually caused several of his cabin mates to become ill and rush from the breakfast table.

One day the counselor overheard some of the campers

discussing a "breakfast date with Teddy." Investigation revealed that on each occasion when Teddy performed the cereal stunt, the boys took Teddy behind the cabin and beat him. Armed with this knowledge the counselor approached Teddy and informed him that he knew about the "breakfast date" and said:

Counselor: "Teddy, if you would just stop spilling that cereal on your head, those guys would quit beating you."
Teddy: (*smiling*) "Yeah, that's right."
Counselor: "Well, doesn't it hurt you when they beat you?"
Teddy: (*still smiling*) "Yeah."
Counselor: "Well?"
Teddy: "Hey, man ... can't you see who is the center of attention ... it's me!"

Obviously this youngster had a serious problem. It took the counselor a long time before he was able to convince Teddy that he could become a vital part of the group without resorting to negative, destructive behavior.

In the classroom setting we see a similar problem in the child who appoints himself the "class clown." Since he has not learned other acceptable methods for effecting entry into the peer group, this child "performs" in silly, bizarre ways.

There are many other behaviors which may indicate the child is limited in knowledge of social approaches which can aid in gaining acceptance by the peer group. The child who becomes the "class gossip," the highly aggressive child, the "class bully" ... these are not problem children in the classical sense; rather they are youngsters who need guidance in developing and perfecting social skills.

In recent years, the peer group has become a powerful influence in the use of drugs and alcohol. Many children report being ostracized by the group if they do not participate in drinking alcohol, using crack, or smoking grass. This type of peer pressure is discussed in Chapter Five.

8. Is the pupil going through a developmental phase?

Sometimes behavior problems are developmental in nature. Refusing to sit at one table (if you are an eight year old boy — and the table is filled with girls) is probably a developmental problem, rather than a disciplinary one.

A three year old experiencing difficulties in sharing may say, "I know we share — but I want it!!" This child may appear to be selfish in the eyes of the adult. But more likely he is involved in the throes of egocentrism and is cognitively unable to perceive that someone else should want the same item he desires. His inability to perceptually imagine the feelings of others makes sharing difficult ... he sees only that he wants the item in question.

Pre-adolescent boys and girls often engage in minor aggressive activity. The boys pick at the girls and push them; the girls hit the boys. In spite of loud voices, vigorous protests and feinted injuries, this activity is usually harmless. Actually one is witnessing early attempts at boy-girl relations — and these initial overtures represent uncultivated preludes of later, more serious relationships. In the middle school and high school one may encounter "teacher baiting." The child purposely resorts to behaviors which will assure a negative response on the part of the teacher. In this situation if the teacher "takes the bait" and verbally attacks the instigator, she creates a minor "folk hero" for the class. Actually an inverse correlation may result — thus the more upset the teacher becomes, the greater the degree of admiration for the child involved.

9. What is the child's image of self?

For many clinicians, this question is the most important. It asks about the child's feelings about himself. It asks — What does the child think when he says, "Who am I; how do I feel about me?" In many ways the first eight questions should give the teacher a reasonably good portrait of the child. Research studies (Purkey, 1978) and clinical evidence show that there is a definite correlation between the student's self-concept and behavior disruption as well as one's academic performance.

The teacher needs to "get inside" the child and know how he feels about himself. Is he defensive? self-centered? withdrawn? does he like himself? Does the child feel like a failure? Teachers should have a repertoire of activities and ideas which can help the child build feelings of confidence. Children need to see that they can achieve; that they can be winners. The child's self-concept is greatly influenced by parental attitudes, teacher-student relationships, peer contacts, and academic success.

Before the Doctor Arrives

In conducting a case study and in gathering data on the specific questions raised in the preceding section, the teacher will often be able to develop a strategy which can help the student change his behavior and the original problem may be solved — or at least improved.

However, there are times when it becomes apparent that the child has a problem or a series of problems which are clearly beyond the scope of the teacher's training. In such situations the teacher should recognize her own limitations and seek outside help. If the teacher must make a referral to the school psychologist, her description and observations will be extremely helpful. In addition to the teacher's child study, the following specific information will be useful to any professional who will ultimately work with the child.

• *To whom does the child relate?* Consider the following relationships and orientation. Person orientation: does he relate better to a particular friend, one parent, a special teacher, only to adults? Object orientation: does he relate primarily to nonhumans;e.g., pets or other animals. Does the child display a preference for reading books, over being with people; would child rather watch TV or play with dolls, blocks rather than other children.

• *How does the child relate?* Leader, follower, dependent, dominant, submissive, hits others, bites others.

• *How is play time used?* Is the use of time creative, destructive, likes only clean activities, messy activities; where is play time spent?

• *What is the child's perception of morality?* Does child know right from wrong? Does the child feel extremely guilty, very tense? Is child over controlled, lack spontaneity?

• *What is the child's orientation to reality?* Could child's views be considered reasonably appropriate, inappropriate? Does child daydream a lot; usually try to avoid reality? Does child lie? Otherwise, seem dazed or out of touch with reality?

• *How does the child communicate?* Is the general approach to others friendly, outgoing as opposed to hostile and angry. Does the child seem to have a chip on his shoulder? Very quiet, non-communicative; absence of any emotion?

• *How does the child feel about himself?* Highly egocentric, defensive, denies problems, regressive; e.g., acts younger than actual age. How does child perceive himself as a person? Does child often say things like, "I am no good; I am bad; I am mean; people do not like me."

Supervisory Conference

When the teacher has determined that the child's problem is clearly beyond her expertise as an educator, she should arrange a conference with her principal or immediate supervisor. Questions which need to be resolved include the following: Who will conference with the parents? What referral suggestions will be made? Who will actually make the referral? Who will follow-up on the referral? What will the teacher's role be during this period?

It is recognized that in some small communities a day care director or private school operator may not have large social agencies available for referral. In these situations we would make the following suggestions of persons or agencies who can advise the private operator on possibilities for referral.

Today, through federal grants, many counties have a mental health clinic or an office of family services. The personnel in these clinics are trained and are happy to help educators with problems. In very small communities, where a mental health center does not exist, the local county health department usually has a person with some training in psychology. Often there is a nurse or psychiatric social worker who can provide referral information.

In addition, there are three other possibilities. In some cases the family may have personal health insurance which utilizes a mental health clinic or other mental health services as part of the insurance plan. If the family does not have their own resources we would suggest you consult your own family physician for referral information. Most family physicians have had some psychiatric training and are knowledgeable concerning available sources of referral in the area. If the family has some religious affiliation, they may wish to seek help from their pastor. Many members of the clergy, particularly young ministers, have received training in pastoral counseling and can provide advice and referral information.

Learning Objectives for Chapter One:

After reading Chapter One, "Will the real problem child please stand up," the reader should be able to:

1. Analyze the extent to which the teacher is creating a discipline problem within the classroom.
2. List child behaviors which are upsetting to the teacher personally.
3. Determine problems from one's own early childhood experiences which may influence and interfere with teaching of young children.
4. Write anecdotal observations in descriptive terms, separating actual behaviors from interpretative comments.
5. List criteria necessary to insure objective observation.
6. Identify physical and psychosocial considerations in normal children which may lead to discipline problems. The text lists nine major considerations; the reader should be able to discuss each consideration and its implications as a potential problem.
7. Determine when a discipline problem is beyond the scope of the educator.
8. Write clinical observations in descriptive terms which can be used by a psychiatrists, psychologist, social worker, or visiting teacher.

Chapter Two

The Double Continuum:
A Different Look at Discipline

Historically, one might view the attitudes of parents and teachers toward discipline as simply a matter of control. For most of history, disciplinary action toward children has been quite strict. In an effort to regulate their behavior, children have been severely beaten, dunked in cold water, deprived of food, burned, abandoned, and even killed. Historians (Borstelmann, 1983) have noted that until the 19th century, most of the world's child population was greatly abused.

The Control Continuum

With the beginning of the child development movement in the latter part of the 19th century, several authorities suggested that strong unreasonable discipline would create severe psychological problems in children. Interestingly, however, during this same period — the Victorian era — a different group of authorities believed that "children should be seen and not heard," and adhered to the maxim of "spare the rod and spoil the child." This was the era when father knew best and ruled the house as an authoritarian figure with a firm hand and a hickory stick. In the years which followed experts have aligned themselves in various positions along a control continuum. Figure 2.1 shows this range of thought.

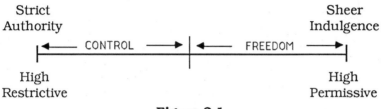

Figure 2.1

Over the years the discipline pendulum has swung back and forth — alternating between the advocates for a strict authoritarian approach and persons suggesting little or no regulation. In the 1920's and 1930's, the Watsonian point of view, with regulated child control and scheduled feeding, was in vogue. In the 1940's, 1950's, and 1960's, the Freudians — along with Dr. Spock, emphasized self-regulation and demand feeding. The late 1960's and 1970's had the flower children who were highly indulgent and felt that everyone should do their own thing. The 1980's had its share of critics who proclaimed, "We need to get tough and get back to basics." Television had programs showing both philosophical approaches and the print media reflected this swing of the pendulum with articles like, "free expression breeds free children," or "let's go back to the woodshed!" and "put the lid on the ID!"

As young professionals we well remember trying to cope with both points of view. Both positions had strong arguments in their favor, but each viewpoint also contained disadvantages. In an article entitled, "Permissiveness Re-examined" (Osborn 1968) the problems with each extreme were examined. The following section is adapted from that article.

Very early in life the child begins to explore his environment by crawling, walking, hitting and knocking over things. During these periods of experimentation it is only human nature that the parent begins to exert pressures in the form of control. By "control pressures" we are referring to such verbal expressions as: "No, not now," "Leave that alone," "I will do that." Control pressures also refers to physical actions like a tap on the hand or an old fashion spanking. Unfortunately, simple control of behavior via techniques of threatening and physical punishment is so simple and expedient, that adults fall into the trap of hollering and hitting for any minor offense. Unless the adult is careful, the child may be surrounded, over-powered may be the better term, by a "Wall of No." Figure 2.2 illustrates the "Wall of No."

Figure 2.2

In the illustration shown in Figure 2.2 we can see that the child is so tightly controlled he cannot express his thoughts and feelings outwardly — he must turn these feelings inward to himself. Psychologists refer to this mechanism of defense as "repression." Confronted with this "Wall of No," the child begins to learn: "I do not have to think, the adults will do my thinking for me." "I cannot say what I feel; I must be bad because I am always wrong in whatever I do." "If I do this, I will get a spanking!" In other words, we get a picture of a child who cannot respond freely — a child who is unable to allow himself to have feelings. *Granted, we have a child who is learning; but we have a child who is learning to respond out of fear of punishment rather than out of understanding of the situation.*

In order to clarify the strict authoritarian system let us use an example. Suppose you have a young child who runs into the street. Under the strict authoritarian mode you would "whale the daylights" out of the child if he ventures near a road or thoroughfare. If the parent performs this spanking without fail, she will have accomplished her objective — at least in part. That is, the child will not go into the street. However, we need to ask, "Why will the child stay out of the street?" It is because of the fear of a spanking, not because of the inherent dangers of playing in the street. This learning works whenever the authority figure is present; but when the authority leaves, and the fear of punishment is removed, the child may dart into the street.

We can see that under such conditions healthy personality development is held back — free expression and autonomy are not allowed to develop. If young children are to explore and discover, they must be allowed to discover their own limitations and learn adequate self-control.

Sheer indulgence

Years ago, the problem of the strict authoritarian approach seemed quite clear. Unfortunately clinical psychologists and teachers often left parents dangling at this point in a discussion on discipline. With the words "free expression" and "real democracy" ringing in their ears, parents often

33

became completely immobilized by any action which would demand an authoritarian stance.

We see this dilemma in the following example. At a recent PTA meeting one of the parents remarked, "Psychologists have told us so much about personality development and the importance of allowing youngsters to express themselves, that I am afraid to do anything for fear I will injure my child's personality." At this same meeting another mother said, "My two year old hits the TV screen with a wooden mallet. I want to stop him but I do not want to hinder this freedom business while he is in this stage of autonomy."

Unfortunately, the course of immobility on the part of the parent or the teacher can be just as damaging to the child as the adult who engages in a strict authoritarian approach. We might use the term "sheer indulgence" to describe this mode of activity. Figure 2.3 shows this behavior.

In Figure 2.3 we see that the child moves freely in any direction without control and without knowledge of the limi-

Figure 2.3

tations which society demands of him. This pattern is as unfortunate as the strict authoritarian position — perhaps even more so, since the child is never made aware of the realistic limits to which he must eventually adjust. If the parent does not present some limiting situations which can enable the child to recognize the demands being placed on him, the child cannot possibly learn to control his feelings. *Learning is almost impossible, and the adult is inviting the child to continually test the situation in a frantic effort to determine if any rules exist.* The child is in for a rude awakening whenever he enters situations which demand rules. Unfortunately, those who finally teach this "untutored child of nature" will not do so in the comfortable understanding way of the parent.

Freedom with control

In considering discipline which is appropriate for children there is a middle ground somewhere between the extremes of "strict authority" and "sheer indulgence." Figure 2.4 illustrates our interpretation of appropriate discipline.

Here we have the original "Wall of No" but now there are openings. In life there are "No's," but in life other alternatives often exist. There is an absolute "No" in hitting the TV set with a mallet. There is no room for "maybe tomorrow" or "perhaps" or "hit it lightly." TV sets cost too much to allow for hammer-hitting types of experimentation. However, there are many acceptable areas where a wooden mallet can be used — on a pounding board, an old dishpan, a piece of wood.

Ideally our "Wall of No" remains firm in areas where it must remain firm; but the "Wall" disappears in areas where freedom can be permitted. Another important consideration in discipline is flexibility. Our "Wall of No" is flexible enough to make allowances for unusual situations which may arise. If bedtime is eight o'clock and special company is expected that evening, then bedtime may be moved to a later hour. Because special occasions arise, flexibility is demanded.

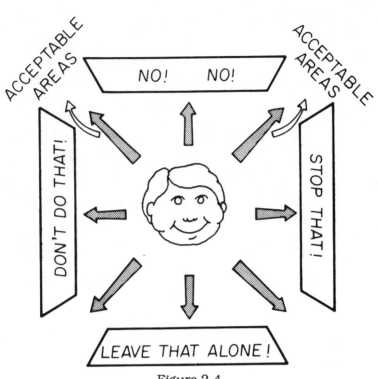

Figure 2.4

We might summarize *freedom with control* in the following manner: Freedom with control has room for both *yes* and *no*; room for change. We would like to emphasize that persons who love their children must discipline them. The child must learn that there are times when a *no* is useful and appropriate. In some situations a prohibition is absolute. There are times when a child needs to be told: "That sort of behavior will not be tolerated in this classroom." No individual — child or adult — can have his or her way all of the time. We like to think of freedom with control as a bank account where we make many deposits of the *yes* nature and a few withdrawals of the *no* nature. When the child moves into situations outside the home and has a good "yes" account, he can withstand the buffeting of "no" which society inevitably provides. With many outlets and many acceptable avenues of entry, the child can accept the avenues which are closed.

36

Freedom with control implies an understanding of children's needs and abilities. This means we do not make demands on youngsters that they are unable to understand. For example, we recognize that young children need to explore feelings of autonomy; to learn the feeling of "I-ness" — to learn they are individuals in their own right. We do not expect youngsters to understand and internalize the concept of sharing until later, when they are less egocentric and capable of understanding the concept of "we-ness." Freedom with control does not mean one capriciously indulges children. Rather it recognizes that young persons are learning to cope in a complex world.

Freedom with control implies learning through understanding rather than learning through fear. For parents and teachers it means making decisions on the important limits and holding to these; while permitting freedom in areas where freedom can be freely given. As adults we want to be informed on the rules and laws which affect us. Children also wish to know the rules of home and society.

A dilemma emerges

Following this philosophical frame of reference we felt that we had a working theory for teaching children in the home and in the classroom setting. If one provided the child with many open avenues for exploration — if one had some definite prohibitions — the child should indeed develop an understanding of self. He should also develop stability, freedom with control, and a healthy realistic approach to society.

In encountering young people and adults our philosophy toward discipline appeared to prove itself. Persons who had been reared under highly strict, rigid conditions — seemed to be rigid, unimaginative and very tough. For example, we remember interviewing one father who pounded his fist on the desk and shouted: "I believe in whipping my children with a strap! They learn to behave or I beat the H____ of them ... " Even the studies by Sears and his associates (1957), confirmed these observations. Their studies had shown that nonaggressive children were those whose parents stopped aggression when it occurred but did not use punitive means to do so. Sears noted that while punishment might stop aggression momentarily — it often generated more hostility in the child.

However, we were confused when we interviewed a number of adults whose experiences ran counter to our theory. We interviewed happy, healthy creative adults who reported that their parents had been strict disciplinarians. And, in spite of being reared in an atmosphere of rather tight control, these persons seemed happy, well-adjusted and content.

On the other hand, we interviewed several adults who had been reared under rather permissive conditions. To our amazement, however, instead of being creative, well-adjusted individuals; these persons appeared uncertain, listless and even hostile. Then, one day, an interesting event occurred on our playground which provided us with some insight into our dilemma.

Ms. Ida Belle, noted for her permissive attitude, was in the yard with a small group of boys. The boys were playing near the gate and finally opened it. (Note: This school was adjacent to a busy street and there was a firm rule against children opening the gate and leaving the playground.) Seeing that Ms. Ida Belle did nothing about their transgression, the boys slowly crept toward the edge of the curb. One child barely escaped being hit. Even as this event unfolded, the teacher did nothing. Suddenly the significance of this observation struck us! Ms. Ida Belle was not really so permissive — she just did not care!

We could label Ms. Ida Belle's method as the "Does Nothing" approach. When following this course of action either the teacher ignores children or simply neglects her duty. The approach of "Does Nothing" reflects an attitude concerning discipline to the child. Sears, et al, reported similar circumstances in their parent interviews on child rearing. They noted that where mothers were often highly tolerant, or careless, in their approach toward undesirable behavior, or the punishment of that behavior; children showed high aggressive outbursts. We felt we were observing the same phenomenon. Thus, it seemed that the control continuum was not sufficient to explain the effects of behavior and control.

In 1959, Shaefer utilized factor analysis to construct a "hypothetical circumplex model of maternal behavior." His model suggested two dimensions for considering discipline. One dimension, "control of autonomy" is similar to our control continuum discussed here; the second dimension was labelled, "love to hostility." This second dimension seemed to add greatly to our understanding of practical discipline as it related to home and classroom and perhaps to solve the dilemma raised in this section.

The Climate Continuum

We felt that Sears' discussion of the tolerant, careless mother; the observation of Ms. Ida Belle and her "Do Nothing" behavior — actually reflected an attitude toward children. These observations, coupled with Shaefer's second dimension, help us raise several questions of great significance for adults who discipline children. These questions include: "What is the emotional climate of the situation in which I mete out control techniques?" "Is my attitude one of warmth and caring; or is my attitude one of ignoring and neglect?" "Do I transmit a feeling that I am accepting or does the child feel I am indifferent?" "Am I cooperative or antagonistic?" "Am I indulgent or indifferent?" In a cassette presentation on discipline (see references) Dunaway discusses a dramatic behavior change in the teacher and the total class when the emotional climate was altered.

Our own teaching experience and observations lead us to firmly believe that children have emotional antennae which can and do receive the feeling tones generated by the teacher. The child quickly learns to determine the emotional climate of the classroom. Since he is physically defenseless against most adults, his own survival may depend upon how well he can accurately assess this climate and its consequences.

Figure 2.5 shows the climate continuum coupled with our original control continuum. The shaded area in Figure 2.5 represents the area in which appropriate discipline can occur. This illustration represents some interesting additions and changes in thinking from the material presented in Figure 2.1.

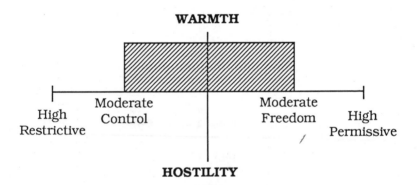

Figure 2.5

The acceptable range of the control continuum has been broadened. This change recognizes that adults can range from moderately strict to moderately permissive and that children can successfully adapt without psychological harm. Until recently, the philosophy surrounding discipline has not been so generous. From the thirties to the mid-seventies, many psychologists, teachers and parents were appalled at any discipline which suggested even the slightest control over children. Note that Figure 2.5 clearly indicates that little or no control is unacceptable. In the late-seventies and the eighties, another group of psychologists and educators moved to the other end of the continuum and suggested a "get tough" and "tough love" attitude toward children. Likewise, Figure 2.5 shows that high control and high restrictive behaviors are inappropriate.

Based on research and clinical findings we are suggesting that a fairly broad "window of acceptability" exists in terms of the control continuum. Parents and teachers should avoid either extreme of "harsh, punitive control" or a "do nothing" attitude. Rather we are stating that the most significant variable in Figure 2.5 is the emotional climate of the home and school in meting out discipline. Thus, the adult should ask: "Is my discipline viewed by the child in an atmosphere of love, warmth and caring?" or "Does the child view my control as the action of a hostile, indifferent adult?"

Thus, we are suggesting that children can tolerate a reasonably wide range of control in the discipline situation. Some parents will be pretty tough with their children; other parents will be fairly easy-going. Some parents will spank their children; others will not. Some teachers will keep their classes quiet and children in their seats; other teachers will tolerate a fair amount of noise and movement. It would seem that in terms of control techniques one's motto should be, "within reason." Children are flexible and can tolerate a reasonable amount of control or a reasonable amount of freedom.

In interviewing adults we often encountered statements such as the following: "My father was really tough ... but he loved us kids." "My teacher really handed out the homework. She wouldn't tolerate any monkey business ... but I really loved math that year." "Our classroom operated at a low level of noise, a medium level of activity, and a high level of love. You wanted to succeed because the teacher wanted you to succeed."

Studies (Brophy & Good, 1974; Goodlad, 1984) clearly show that the teacher, and the climate she creates, can make a difference. Areas such as the quality of the pupil-teacher relationship, student involvement in decision making, teacher expectations are all important. The classic study by Rosenthal and Jacobson (1968) showed that the teacher's expectations of a student's performance became a self-fulfilling prophecy.

Children can and do learn under a reasonably wide range of conditions. Subjecting them to extremes in behavior control can make learning more difficult and even harmful. However, the key question is not one of control. It is the teacher's attitude — the climate for learning which she creates in the classroom. The teacher can create an atmosphere of apathy, and non-caring or a climate of love, warmth, and understanding.

Learning Objectives For Chapter Two:

After reading Chapter Two, "A double continuum: A new look at discipline," the reader should be able to:

1. Define and describe the control continuum in discipline.
2. Compare several discipline approaches ranging from authoritarian to indulgent and cite the effects of learning via these strategies.
3. Define and describe the emotional climate continuum.
4. Compare discipline approaches in terms of the "classroom climate" and cite the effects via these strategies.
5. Identify a workable approach to discipline in terms of both child control and emotional climate.

Chapter Three

How Children Learn

Let us consider some of the ways in which behavior is learned. Most activities are the result of learned behavior — solving a puzzle, holding a paint brush, bathing a doll, dressing oneself — all represent behaviors which are learned. Biting, hitting, pinching, kicking, and smoking marijuana are also examples of behaviors which have been learned.

The Role of Drives

We might ask a very basic question. Why do people behave at all? Early learning theorists said that behavior resulted because of basic drive reduction, and learning occurred in connection with the reduction of these basic drives. These drives were called primary or innate drives since they were basic to life itself. For example, if an individual was sufficiently hungry or thirsty, he would be forced to respond to these drives — just as a matter of mere survival, and this action would reduce the drive.

However, in reducing the drive, the individual learns something related to drive reduction. For example, if a person was very thirsty, he would quickly learn that water, as opposed to food, would reduce this specific primary drive.

Later other psychologists discussed social drives. However, these drives were not innate; rather, they appeared to be the result of learned behavior. For example, the need for approval, praise, recognition and affection were viewed as social in nature. Like the primary drives, these social forces could motivate the individual to respond.

More recently social psychologists have added exploring and curiosity as meaningful drives which can motivate. For example, in work with animals who were not thirsty or hungry there remained, nevertheless, a tendency to move about and explore. We also see this behavior in the well fed, satisfied baby. He kicks his feet, moves his head, explores his hands and generally exhibits a curious mode of behavior.

Thus we see, *a drive is created as a result of some need.* As the need increases, it creates a tension system within the individual which will finally move him to action. This tension system can be the result of a primary (innate) drive such as hunger or thirst; a secondary (learned) drive, such as the desire for recognition or approval; or an activity (curiosity) drive such as the desire for additional stimulation. These drives motivate the individual to perform some activity which will reduce the tension system.

The Role of Reinforcement

It is generally believed that when a drive is reduced, learning will occur. The event or circumstance which reduces or alters the drive is termed *reinforcement.* A general rule concerning reinforcement is as follows: *Whenever a response is reinforced — there is a greater likelihood that the response will occur again.*

There are two types of reinforcement: Positive and negative. Positive reinforcements are pleasant stimuli such as a smile, praise, candy or gaining attention. For our purposes we will also refer to a positive reinforcement as a reward. Whenever these events occur, the child is most likely to repeat the behaviors which produced these pleasant stimuli.

In negative reinforcement an unpleasant stimulus is *removed* in order to encourage (or strengthen) a given type of behavior. Since this concept is usually difficult for teacher to grasp, let us provide an example of negative reinforcement: A child is talking to his neighbor in class and the teacher scolds the child for talking. The child will probably stop talking and the teacher will stop scolding. In this example his cessation of talking has been strengthened since the teacher stopped scolding.

Generally speaking, negative reinforcement is quicker and more effective than positive reinforcement in establishing new behaviors. However, it is almost impossible to create unpleasant situations which will provide negative reinforcers which are not, at the same time, either inherently harmful, inappropriate or very unpleasant to the child.

A third concept which is useful in our discussion is *punishment.* Many persons assume that punishments and negative reinforcements are synonymous terms — however, many psychologists distinguish some subtle differences between the two concepts. Ambron (1981, p.151) illustrates these differences quite well with the following definitions: "In negative reinforcement an unpleasant stimulus is *removed* in order to *encourage* a particular response. In *punishment* an unpleasant or painful stimulus is *applied*, in order to *discourage* a given kind of behavior."

In our discussion we will refer to the concept of punishment and various forms of punishment which may be applied in order to discourage certain behaviors. For our purposes let us designate three categories of punishing behaviors: physical, verbal, and ignoring. These approaches will be detailed in later sections of this chapter. However, we do wish to make several observations about the general concept of punishment and its role in changing behavior.

We agree with ACEI's position paper (Cryan, 1987) on corporal punishment. ACEI, along with many other major national organizations, including NAEYC and the PTA, have proposed the banning of corporal punishment in all child care, school and other educative settings. Corporal punishment is unnecessary and can cause physical and psychological damage to children. Hyman and Wise (1979, p. 4) give the definition for corporal punishment as, "the infliction of pain by a teacher or other educational officials upon the body of the student as a penalty for doing something which has been disapproved by the punisher."

One of the seductive qualities of corporal punishment is that it appears to work immediately. For example, if a child is spanked, he usually stops the behavior which caused him to receive the spanking. However, the teacher should recognize that this cessation of behavior may be only temporary. In many situations the child may learn ways to avoid the punishment — without changing the original behavior. For example, the child may wait until the teacher is not looking — or out of the room — and then repeat the behavior, because the fear of punishment has been removed. In addition, physical punishment preempts better means of communicating with a child and teaches, by personal example, that inflicting pain on others is permissible. It is also damaging in the sense that it narrows the teacher's options and tunnels her vision and image as a scholar.

Usually punishment, *per se*, has little meaningful long term educational value. Punishment may show that the teacher is very unhappy, but it seldom provides the child with acceptable alternatives. The teacher should recognize that in order to make the total learning experience successful, she must show the child acceptable ways of behaving — or appropriate ways to change his behavior.

Positive reinforcement can generally be provided in three ways: token, activity or social. Token reinforcement — that is giving the child a piece of candy, food, a gold star, stamps, stickers, money, or a toy. Activity reinforcement — that is allowing the child the opportunity to engage in an activity of his own choosing, which he enjoys very much. Social reinforcement — that is praising the child or complimenting him or paying attention to a particular bit of behavior.

Generally token reinforcement will cause young children to respond most quickly in terms of behavior change. While token reinforcement usually works faster, it is not necessarily the most effective in the long run. As a general rule, the authors personally do not care to use token reinforcement under normal classroom conditions. It is recognized, however, that there are times when the teacher may feel a small token reinforcement is necessary to help enhance learning. In these situations, we would suggest that the tokens be used sparingly. Too often teachers fall into the "token trap". They wear smocks with kangaroo pockets and pop M&M's into each waiting mouth. At the beginning of the year the reward may be a small portion of candy. However, as the year progresses, the teacher continues to increase the rewards and "token inflation" occurs. In using tokens, the teacher should endeavor to help the child learn to work for intrinsic rewards and actually decrease the tokens over time.

Our own experience has been that, under regular classroom conditions, children usually do not need coins or candy. Most children learn quite effectively via activity and social types of reinforcement. The opportunity to enjoy a preferred activity can be a powerful reinforcer. Appendices B and D will help teachers determine activities which are of interest to a specific child.

We feel that attention and praise can be the most powerful reinforcers for the teacher. However, these social reinforcers should be given in ways which will ultimately encourage intrinsic motivation. Brophy (1982) points out that rather than merely reinforcing behavior, praise can effectively teach students how to think about their own actions. He states that effective praise should be delivered contingently and specify the particulars of an accomplishment. Praise should show spontaneity, variety, and credibility as well as provide students with information about their own competence. It should be given in recognition of noteworthy efforts and accomplishments and focus the students' attention on their own task-relevant behavior.

Brophy points out that ineffective praise is unsystematic, random and diffuse. It shows bland uniformity and rewards mere participation without consideration for effective performance. It does not provide students with definite information about their status and without regard for the effort expended. Finally, it focuses attention on the teacher as an external authority figure who is manipulating them.

There are several ways by which undesirable behavior can be terminated. Ignoring the undesired behavior, taking away an item, removing an item, not giving token reinforcement, removing the child from the situation (generally called, "time out"), and physical punishment. In most instances the authors have found that ignoring behavior is the best way to terminate an activity. However, there are times when ignoring undesirable behavior will not be effective. In some cases, ignoring a specific behavior may lead to escalation of the behavior and contagion to other members of the class. In these situations, the teacher needs to move promptly and and firmly.

Classical and Operant Conditioning

Learning theorists believe there are two major forms of learning: classical and operant conditioning.

Classical Conditioning

The first studies on classical conditioning were performed on dogs by the Russian psychologist, Pavlov. When a neutral item (a bell) was rung at the same time the animal received food, an association or connection was established. After a short number of trials the animal would salivate upon hearing the bell. Under these circumstances, learning had taken place — the bell caused the dog to salivate.

This learned reflex is called a conditioned reflex ... that is, a previously neutral item, the bell, has taken on some drive value. Or, in simpler terms, the bell motivated the dog to respond.

It is believed that much simple learning takes place in this fashion. Psychologists believe that emotional learning takes place via classical conditioning. For example, a young child may make unpleasant connections (associations) between the physician's office and receiving a shot. In some instances children are known to begin to fear all persons in offices or all persons wearing white.

Good feelings can also become associated in a similar fashion. The general good feeling one gets from viewing a lake or a sunset ... these good feelings develop from associations made through classical conditioning.

Operant Conditioning

The concept of operant conditioning was developed by B. F. Skinner in the 1930's. One major difference between classical and operant conditioning is the sequence of the stimulus and the response. In classical conditioning the subject's response *follows* the stimulus. In the Pavlovian experiment, the dog salivated *after* seeing the food or hearing the bell. In operant conditioning the response *precedes* the reward. In Skinner's experiments with pigeons, the pigeon pressed a lever and *then* he received a pellet of food. Receiving this pellet of food is termed a *positive reinforcement* (a reward).

In a classic study Reingold, et al, used operant conditioning to encourage vocalizations in young infants. The experimenters rewarded random vocalizations of three month old infants by smiling and cooing. Within one week there was a statistically significant increase in the vocalizations of the infants. Later, when the rewards (smiling and cooing) were terminated, the vocalizations returned to their earlier level.

Skinner's theory of reinforcement states that a person develops a certain behavior via a number of small approximations. As the skill in performing a certain behavior improves, the individual consolidates his repertoire. He retains the correct responses, which are positively reinforced, and "drops out" the incorrect responses, since they are negatively reinforced.

An example of this phenomenon can be seen by observing a child solve a wooden puzzle. The first time he attempts to put the puzzle together he makes many false moves. Since these movements do not aid in putting the puzzle together they are, in effect negatively reinforced. The movements which result in completing a portion of the puzzle are positively reinforced. After the child has successively solved the puzzle a number of times, his movements are smooth; mistakes are fewer.

Techniques for Changing Behavior

Research shows that the teacher can effect changes in behavior by making use of the principles of reinforcement theory. The application of this theory is called behavior modification. By utilizing this theory the teacher can help the student: a) strengthen and maintain appropriate behaviors; b) weaken and/or extinguish behaviors which are inappropriate; and c) teach new patterns of behavior which will be helpful to the child. Several suggestions and specific techniques are presented in this section and in Appendices A, B, and D. In most cases, if the teacher will utilize these techniques in a consistent manner and follow the specific suggestions outlines below the child will change his behavior.

1. *Observe the child carefully.*

The value of observation cannot be overemphasized. Chapter One discussed the importance of the case study and presented some specific suggestions for observation. Prior to instituting the techniques for behavior change, observe the child's behavior in the classroom setting. We once had a child who solved all his problems by fighting. We later learned that his father had emphasized that boys who would not fight were "sissies." The father would give his son a quarter each time he "stood up and fought" for his rights. This dual combination of social and token reinforcement had its effect. The youngster soon became the class bully.

When observing a specific piece of behavior establish some baseline data. For example, let us assume you have a child who is hitting. In gathering baseline data the following questions would be helpful: Determine the frequency of the behavior: "How many times a day does the hitting occur?" Determining the timing of the behavior: "When does the hitting occur — throughout the day; just before lunch; early in the morning?" Determine the situations in which hitting occurs: "What are the circumstances under which the hitting happens — to get toys, to share, only in the block corner?" What people are involved? "Only hits girls; will only hit specific children."

Actually these types of baseline data are rather easy to collect. Record the events and circumstances in a notebook, on a clipboard, or use index cards. These data can be quite simple and to the point — for example:

    9:04   Edris hit Burma. Said he wanted her trike.
    10:10 Edris hit Burma during snack time. Said she took
           all the crackers.
    11:42 Edris hit Burma during storytime. Said she took
           his book.

Our example of three items could provide the teacher with

several additional questions. She might ask, "Does Edris only hit Burma?" "What happens just prior to the hitting behavior—what set it off?" "Does Burma actually provoke the hitting behavior?" "Does Edris know how to share — how to respond in positive ways?"

As the teacher gathers additional baseline data she will be able to answer the questions of behavior frequency and determine situational variables. The writers have known teachers who gathered baseline data on several children simultaneously using this technique.

In gathering these data the teacher will also ascertain areas which are important to the child. If the teacher is to use reinforcement, she must know the child's interests sufficiently to determine areas and activities which can serve as reinforcers. Appendix B offers suggestions on constructing an "Interest Finder" chart.

2. Decide on the behavior to be changed and set attainable goals.

Ronald, age five, was a very talkative child. During discussion periods Ronald dominated the conversation, seldom allowing anyone else to talk. Initially the teacher did not set her goal to "keep Ronald quiet for ten minutes." Rather she established a goal of one minute. In changing behavior, the teacher must design success experiences which children can achieve. Whenever Ronald met this goal during discussion period the teacher praised him. As time passed the teacher lengthened the interval before giving praise for "quiet behavior." After a few weeks Ronald, while still talkative, allowed others to share in the discussion period.

3. Reward the behavior you wish to maintain.

We need to reverse our thinking patterns. Instead of waiting to pounce on bad behavior; we need to catch the child

52

in the act of doing something good. Then, in order to maintain the "good" behavior, we reinforce it.

For example: Ms. Feldman was having trouble at juice time. Some children were neglecting to clean up. Ms. Feldman noticed that each day she was repeating the same admonitions: "Noreen, pick up your napkin ... Desi, wipe up you spill ... Wayne, where did you put your juice glass?"

After examining her own actions, Ms. Feldman decided to reward only the behavior she wished to maintain. She waited until the child made a correct response and said, "Noreen, thank you for putting your napkin in the waste basket... Desi, I see you wiped up your spill ... " Ms. Feldman also noticed her own attitude began to change. Instead of nagging, she found that rewarding behavior was both more effective and more satisfying. Rather than punishing children when they were deviant, she rewarded children for appropriate behavior.

Social reinforcers are usually adequate in most classroom settings. Praising a child, looking into his eyes, smiling, nodding, patting the child on the back, sitting next to the child, placing the child in your lap — these are powerful reinforcing agents. Appendix A offers many suggestions for social reinforcers.

There are also times when the teacher may wish to use an activity as a reinforcing agent. Through utilizing an interest chart, see Appendix B, the teacher can determine "natural reinforcers" — e. g., reinforcers which have a special meaning for the student. By utilizing a social or an activity reinforcer at the appropriate time, the teacher can effectively reward the behavior she wishes to maintain.

4. Ignore the behavior you wish to discourage.

Behavior which precedes a reward is strengthened. For example, Dottie, age two, is crying. Mother gives Dottie a piece of candy and says, "That's a good girl." A few days later Dottie has a temper tantrum and again mother gives her a piece of candy to stop crying. Unknowingly the mother is reinforcing the behavior (crying) which she actually wishes to terminate. Over the long haul, the mother would do better if she ignored this behavior, thereby teaching Dottie that crying would not "pay off," that is, be rewarded.

Ignoring can be a very powerful tool. Often the child is employing negative behavior in order to gain the attention of the adult. The act of ignoring takes away the mechanism which is being used as an attention getting device.

This suggestion is easier to state than to implement. However, most behavior can be ignored, without serious consequences. Our own experience and observation is that teachers have difficulty in being patient over a long period of time. They often expect the undesired behavior to stop the first few times it is ignored. However, if the behavior has been successful for months — or even years — it will take time before the behavior will become extinguished.

One second grade teacher, Ms. Morgan, had an entire table which continued to be noisy and disruptive. After observing Ms. Morgan several days it was obvious that many of her approaches to this table were for the sole purpose of restoring quiet. The observer even noted that children at other tables were beginning to become involved in excessive movement, handwaving and hollering to gain the teacher's attention. One Monday Ms. Morgan announced to the class that she planned to spend her time with table groups which were quiet and prepared to utilize her services. Note: In another section of the book we will see the value of this technique — clarity. The teacher is making clear the rules of the situation.

Following this announcement, Ms. Morgan would move to a table only when the children were working. In the case of the disruptive table, Ms. Morgan was particularly alert. When this table assumed an attitude of study she provided both verbal ("Now you are working quietly, that's fine.") and physical (patting a child, squeezing a hand, etc.) reinforcement.

Within a few days — by ignoring the noisy groups and involving herself with children showing performance behaviors she wished continued, the noise level of the entire class has been reduced significantly.

5. *Reinforce incompatible behavior.*

In addition to rewarding the behavior she wishes to maintain, the teacher can use the technique of rewarding incompatible behavior. In our previous example, Ms. Morgan employs this technique when she notes: "Now you are working quietly, that's fine." In this instance quiet behavior is incompatible with noisy behavior.

To use another illustration: If you wish to discourage running — ignore the running behavior but reward non-running. For example: "Ashley, I am pleased to see you are walking." "Josh, I am happy to see that you are sitting at the table."

6. *Recognize that some negative reinforcers and punishments may be positive!*

Periodically a teacher will state that a negative reinforcer or a punishment has no effect. There are situations, however, when a reinforcing stimulus "appears" to be negative — but, in actual fact, the overall impact of the reinforcing stimulus creates a positive effect on the child.

For example, a teacher reprimands a child after he spills paint on the table. If the child spilled the paint in order to get attention or get to clean up the mess instead of work which the child would like to avoid, the reprimand will serve as a positive reinforcement instead of a punishment. Situations can arise in the older elementary grades, middle and high school in which an older child may be "punished" by the teacher but "rewarded" by the peer group. For example, the class clown may perform an act which is annoying to the teacher. The teacher gets upset and admonishes the youngster. After class, however, the peer group may approach the child who misbehaved and say, "Hey, man, that was really funny! You really bugged that old teacher!!" Thus the child may be positively reinforced when the teacher admonishes him — because he is receiving attention and praise from the peer group.

Attention *per se*, is a powerful reinforcer. Our observations show that hitting and biting often fall into this category. It is almost impossible to ignore biting behavior — thus biting is always noticed, always commented upon; often unwittingly positively reinforced.

7. Reinforcement should be immediate.

An important aspect of learning, particularly with young children, is to have the reward follow closely behind the appropriate response. If the teacher has assessed correctly what is important to the child and rewards him immediately for behaviors which approximate the desired response, she will get behavior change. Unfortunately teachers often handle the situation in a haphazard fashion and are too casual in terms of praise and approval. Remember that when a child is ignored (even by accident) this ignoring can have the effect of punishment. After new behavior patterns have been established, reinforcement can be intermittent.

Timing of punishment is an important consideration. Walters, Parke, and Cane (1965) theorize that the timing of discipline may be related to shame and guilt. In an experiment these authors timed their punishment in two ways: (a) just prior to playing with a forbidden item and (b) after the child had already begun to play with the item. The results of the study suggested that children punished under condition (a) were more likely to resist future temptation than the children punished under condition (b). One possible explanation might be that early punishment aids in building superego feelings (feelings of conscience). We can observe this situation when a small child contemplates touching a forbidden object but reprimands himself saying, "No, no!"

In situations where punishment is administered "after the crime" we might theorize that the child experiences feelings of shame coupled with fear of discovery and reprisal. In the nursery school one can observe this psychological "battle" occurring within the young child. For example:

Terrance and Paul are playing in the block corner. They are building a ship to take them to the "North Pole in Alabama." Terrance reaches for a large cylinder block but Paul grabs it first. Terrance pushes Paul. Paul turns and starts to hit Terrance with the block. For a moment he stops, shakes his head and says, really to himself, "No, no." He resists striking Terrance for a few seconds — then suddenly hits him with the block. After hitting Terrance, Paul immediately scans the room to see if any adults are watching. Terrance starts to cry and says, "Bad boys hit!"

In this example of early socialization we can observe Paul feels guilty — at least pangs of conscience — as he considers whether or not he should strike Terrance. After losing the battle with the superego he becomes afraid that some adult may punish him for his transgression. Further reinforcement of these feelings of shame occur when Terrance says, "Bad boys hit!"

While it is impossible to immediately reinforce behavior on every occasion, delayed reinforcement is feasible with older children. In situations where punishment must be delayed it can still be effective if the adult talks with the child and explains the nature of the wrong doing and the proposed punishment. The adult can also help the older child learn to search for alternate solutions which can be self-regulating and yet satisfying.

8. Reinforcement is contingent upon the desired response.

Suggestion seven points out the importance of timing as it is coupled with the reinforcement. Timing is crucial but, unfortunately, some adults provide positive reinforcement in anticipation of the desired response. For example the teacher may say, "I will read you a story and then we will clean up our mess." Likewise, it is easy for parents to fall into this trap. For example: "You may play now, if you will do your homework later."

Becker (1971, p. 25) refers to this problem and states: "To teach a child to carry out his responsibilities, require the less preferred activity to come before the more preferred activity." This postulate is generally referred to as *Grandma's law:* "You do what I want you to do, before you get to do what you want to do."

Thus, the teacher should employ activities which the child likes, to reinforce an activity which has less appeal to the child. For example: "When the blocks are picked up, you may paint at the easel." "After we finish our arithmetic assignment, I have a surprise for the class." Appendix B offers some suggestions which may help the teacher determine preferred activities for children. Grandma's law is really the heart of contingency management. That is, after the individual has performed a specific task, he can engage in an activity that he enjoys.

To effectively utilize Grandma's law we would suggest the following: The teacher can make a list with two columns. On the left side write the preferred activities; on the right side, list the necessary, but least preferred activities. For example:

High Preference	Low Preference
Reading book	Finishing math problems
Playing a game	Studying spelling words
Using computer	Contributing to class discussion
Feeding fish	Copying sentences from the board

For example: Carmen enjoyed working puzzles but did not like to do arithmetic problems. The teacher made an agreement with Carmen that after she solved ten problems, she could work one puzzle. Carmen began to happily work on the arithmetic, knowing that later she could play with a puzzle. Most children are willing to work for the privilege of later engaging in a preferred activity. It is imperative that the teacher follow through with her promise when it is made, otherwise she is inconsistent.

9. Reinforcement, initially, should be continuous.

Let us discuss the nature of continuous and intermittent reinforcement. In establishing behavior change, the reinforcement must be continuous. Unfortunately teachers are often too casual when they are endeavoring to establish behavior change. If the teacher decides to reward a specific behavior, she must initially do it continuously if the change is to take place.

Example: A nursery school teacher is trying to encourage Randy to use fingerpaint. Randy gingerly places one finger in the paint. T: "Isn't that fun?" (Randy smiles faintly.) T: "Here try the paint" (shows Randy the paper.) Randy tentatively touches the paint on the paper. At this moment the teacher gets distracted and moves across the room to converse with the assistant. Randy, meantime, makes a wide sweeping movement with his finger and succeeds in painting a lovely red streak across the paper. Randy looks up, smiles and hollers: "Teacher, look!" The teacher remains involved with her assistant. Randy looks at his finger, frowns and retreats to the bathroom and washes his hands. About ten minutes later the teacher returns to Randy; invites him to fingerpaint – he refuses. Unless reinforcement is continuous, it is difficult to effect change. Once the behavior is established, however, reinforcement can be intermittent and the new behavior will maintain itself.

Please note that the reverse holds true. Thus, if you wish to stop an undesired piece of behavior, punishment or negative reinforcers must likewise be continuous. If the stimuli are presented in a haphazard and unpredictable fashion, the undesired behavior will still maintain itself and change will not take place. This situation can occur when the adult holds firm most of the time; but occasionally gives in or ignores the misbehavior.

Example: Janice always runs in the school hallway. We observe that Janice is periodically reprimanded for running; however, this behavior is generally ignored by the teacher. We predict that Janice will continue running (which she obviously enjoys — it is highly positive experience for her) since the overall reinforcement pattern is positive. We are correct in our prediction.

10. *Reinforcement should be consistent.*

One of the most difficult tasks in supervision is to get beginning teachers to be consistent. Consistency is usually a big problem with parents. One can accidently create bad habits in children by alternating between being firm and giving in. When teachers or parents are inconsistent, learning appropriate behavior is difficult. It is like having the rules of a game constantly changed. Generally parents and teachers are inconsistent in areas where they themselves are uncertain. This uncertainty is transferred to the child.

The best example of inconsistency we remember occurred in a children's summer camp. Harold, the camp counselor for the eleven year old boys, was experiencing difficulty in getting his campers to bed. One night one of our observers recorded the following:

Harold (*shouting*) "All right, you guys — this is the third time I am going to say, 'This is the last time to get to bed!'" The boys continued their rough housing. Four minutes pass.

Harold (*shouting*) "All right, you guys, — I *really* mean it this time ... this is the *fourth* time I am going to say, 'This is the

this time ... this is the *fourth* time I am going to say, 'This is the *last time* to get to bed!'"

Several minutes pass. The boys engage in a pillow fight. Bill hits Irv over the head and Irv starts to cry. Harold goes over to comfort Irv.

Harold (*shouting*) "All right, you guys ... . See what happens when you fight! Now this is the *fifth* time I am going to say, 'This is the *last time* to get to bed.'" This pronouncement is greeted with hooting and yelling.

The next day we overheard two of the campers in a discussion. One said, "I will bet you a candy bar that tonight Harold will say, 'This is the *sixth time...*'" The other camper responded, "It's a bet!"

Please note that the campers are learning quite well. Unfortunately, they are not learning the rules which concern bedtime. Rather they have learned that rough housing, fighting and shouting types of behavior delay the unpleasant process of going to bed. By creating disturbances they are able to stay up later each evening. In addition, "bugging the counselor" becomes a rewarding experience — as the campers see they can completely confound this representative of the adult world.

11. *Re-observe the child and evaluate goals.*

Once you set your goals for a child and decide on the behaviors you wish to reinforce, keep a record. Each day the teacher should study her observational materials to determine if her reinforcement are meeting the criteria set forth in this chapter. For example: Are the reinforcements appropriate for the particular child or group you are attempting to modify? Are the reinforcements clear, consistent and appropriately timed? Under what conditions do the reinforcements take place? How do the children respond? Based on this new information, what changes should be made in teaching strate-

Implementing Reinforcement Theory:

Case #1. Charlie. Several years ago a friend was teaching in a ghetto area. She had a five year old boy who was extremely quiet and withdrawn. After observing him for several days the teacher noticed the child arrived earlier than the other pupils. Her initial observations follow:

T: "Good morning Charlie."
C: (no reply)
T: "How are you this morning?"
C: (looks non-committal at T.)

Each morning the conversation followed a similar pattern. The teacher would comment on the weather. Charlie's clothing, plans for the day — but no topic seemed to interest the youngster. Learning that Charlie had a dog, the teacher was able to use this knowledge as the following exchange shows:

T: "Good morning Charlie."
C: (nothing)
T: "How is your dog this morning?"
C: (faint smile, shrugs shoulders)
T: "I don't believe I know your dog's name."
C: "Ringo."
T: "Ringo, Hey that's a great name for a dog. I'll bet you are good friends."

Through rewarding his comments and showing a genuine interest the teacher helped Charlie to talk more. As the conversation increased the teacher was able to discover other areas of interest. By mid-year, Charlie was able to converse better and share with others.

Case # 2. Christopher. Ms. Markette, fourth grade teacher, noticed that Christopher had great difficulty in finishing his work. He seemed to wander around the room generally disrupting class. Ms. Markette was unable to find anything which would hold Christopher's attention for more than a few minutes.

One day during the outdoor play period, Christopher led the first grade boys in kickball. He taught the boys the rules and generally assumed a leadership role in the game. It was apparent that everyone was having a good time.

Upon returning indoors, Ms. Markette received a note from the kindergarten teacher requesting some temporary help for her class. Remembering the outside events, Ms. Markette sent Christopher to help in the kindergarten. Thirty minutes later Christopher returned to the room — all smiles. When questioned he said he would like to help again stating, "Teaching those little kids is a lot of fun!"

On the following day Christopher began to disturb the class. Ms. Markette said, "Christopher, if you can sit quietly at your seat and complete your work, I will let you help in the kindergarten." Note that the teacher is utilizing suggestion number eight, Gramdma's law. Reinforcement is contingent upon the desired response.

Over the next few weeks Christopher was rewarded for work behavior. In the meantime the kindergarten teacher reported that he was a great help and well liked by the kindergarten children. She, too, praised Christopher for his efforts. As time progressed, Christopher attended more to his work and wandering aimlessly about the room almost completely stopped.

Case #3. Debra. Debra talked so loudly her voice reverberated down the hall. Her loud voice carried easily and disturbed the reading groups. After determining the problem was not physiological and that hearing acuity was in the normal range, her first grade teacher devised the following strategy.

The teacher told Debra that her voice was too loud and was disturbing others. Using a TV set as an analogy, the teacher explained that Debra needed to "turn down the volume." The teacher added: "To remind you, I will 'pretend' to turn the volume down on your voice. " The teacher then gave a visual demonstration of turning down a volume knob. Debra laughed and said, "Oh!, I see! Whenever you turn your hand I will lower my voice."

Later in class when Debra's voice became loud, the teacher would give Debra a visual cue. In addition, when Debra did talk in a quiet voice, the teacher would nod and smile. Within two weeks Debra was speaking in a normal voice.

Case #4. Sam. One year a teacher approached the authors concerning one of her four year old pupils. Following suggestion #1 we observed the child (Sam) for one week to establish baseline data. We found several interesting things:

• Sam bit or hit someone an average of 23 times a day!

• It was obvious that the hitting behavior was highly rewarding. Other classmates quickly gave in to Sam's demands — if he wanted an item — he got it.

• In many instances, as one might suspect, when Sam approached other children they would run away.

• The teachers were often inconsistent whenever Sam hit or bit another child. At different times during the week the teachers had ignored Sam, physically restrained him, argued with him, threatened him, removed him from the situation.

• Observations also indicated that most of the adult contacts (the teacher and two assistants) were negative in nature — restraining Sam, reproaching Sam, etc. During this period we observed an interesting incident. One of the assistant teachers was playing Looby Loo with the children. Our observation is as follows:

Teacher: "Here we go Looby-Loo ... Sam, hold Darlene's hand... Here we go Looby-Lie ... Sam, will you leave Mary alone ... Here we go Looby-Loo... Sam, will you leave Mary alone ... Here we go Looby — SAM STOP! — Loo..."

Sadly, the assistant had nothing positive to say to Sam and we observed nineteen prohibitions during this single situation! Clearly this circumstance, coupled with Sam's biting behavior, demanded action.

After much discussion several decisions were made. 1) We would use a time out technique and remove Sam to a nearby room. 2) Whenever Sam bit a child the teacher would say in a firm and definite voice that the behavior was inappropriate and would not be allowed to continue. 3) The teacher would remove Sam from the room as expeditiously, and as matter-of-factly, as possible. In other words we did not want the teacher to engage in a fight or argument with Sam — rather to clearly point out the misbehavior and remove him from the room. 4) The teacher would place Sam in another room saying, "When you can calm down and play with other children, you may return to the group." The time out room was a well-lighted storage room, sixteen feet square. The room was cleared of most of the boxes and two small chairs were placed in the room. There was a small window in the door. It was agreed that if, at any time, Sam was frightened or did not calm down within four minutes the teacher would enter the room, comfort and calm him. It was also agreed that initially, because of Sam's volatile behavior, if he was calm for ten seconds, the teacher would open the door, smile and compliment Sam on his calm, quiet behavior and announce that he could return to the room. The teacher would also comment on the importance of trying to play with others without having to bite or hit. 5) A complete record would be kept of Sam's hitting and biting behavior including type and time the behavior occurred; the circumstance, and the amount of time spent in the time out room.

Note: We would like to make a statement about the time out procedure. It can be effective in modifying behavior, but the technique can also be abused. Time out is a method of removal and, in our opinion, it should be used only when a child has clearly demonstrated he is unable to function in the group. In a preschool or primary school setting the time out procedure should usually be conducted in the classroom. For example, the child may be placed in a chair, away from other children for a short period of time. A preferred method would be to place the child in a quiet part of the room — where he may be removed from the children, but not totally restricted. As a rule of thumb, the maximum length of time a child should be placed in a time out setting should be one minute for each year of age. Thus, the maximum for a three year old would be three minutes; a four year old four minutes, etc. The maximum amount of time for any youngster, regardless of age, should not exceed six to eight minutes. A kitchen timer can be set for three or four minutes. Then, when the child hears the buzzer, he can return to the group on his own. The intent of this technique is to give the child the opportunity to calm down and to understand the reason for his removal. In some cases a child may need assistance in returning to the group. A friendly remark by the teacher can ease the transition. Clewett (1988) discusses some of the shortcomings inherent in using the time out technique and points out some of the potential emotional problems which can occur when this technique is abused.

In Sam's case, because of the severity of the hitting and biting, we felt it was necessary to remove him from the playroom. While in the time out room, he was under constant observation. The longest Sam ever stayed in the room was two minutes, 34 seconds. Figure 3.1 shows a complete record of the bitting and hitting behavior.

Figure 3.1 shows that during the week when baseline data were obtained, Sam averaged 23 aggressive responses per day! On the first day the "time out" procedure was employed, Sam's biting and hitting dropped to an N=8 times. (Denoted as "x" on the graph.) Figure 3.1 shows the number of aggressive responses continued to decline during the ensuing weeks. By the fourth week the biting had stopped and the hitting behavior had declined to one or two transgressions per day.

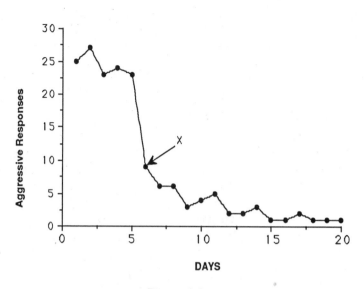

Figure 3.1

In addition to utilizing the time out technique, we worked with the teachers in an effort to determine areas where Sam could be positively reinforced for appropriate behavior. One of Sam's favorite activities was playing the the sandbox. The teachers took special pains to pay attention to Sam and comment that he could play successfully without resorting to biting or hitting. During the first week, through intensive observation, the teachers were able to discover several other activities which Sam enjoyed and to reward him whenever appropriate behavior occurred. The teachers also began to ascertain "potential problem situations" and moved to redirect Sam before a problem arose. Whenever possible, the teachers tried to anticipate Sam's behavior and give him a warning prior to a hitting or biting episode. As Figure 3.1 shows, the biting and hitting behavior lessened significantly over time. Coupled with the decrease, Sam began to develop more appropriate social responses.

During this period Sam also began receiving positive reinforcers from some of his classmates. As the hitting and biting diminished, several children became friendly with Sam and actively sought him as a playmate. Interestingly, however, we felt the biggest change had occurred with the adults in the group. As they observed positive reinforcement working effectively, they became more conscious of their contacts with other children.

Reinforcement is not a panacea; it will not solve all behavior problems. Reinforcement is one way in which children learn; it can be an effective tool when used wisely by the teacher. Understanding the principles of reinforcement will help the teacher in modifying behavior.

Some Thoughts on Assertive Discipline

Assertive discipline employs reinforcement strategies and utilizes many techniques which are discussed in this chapter. Since a number of school systems employ a program called, "Assertive Discipline," (Canter, 1976) we would like to make a few comments concerning this approach toward classroom management. It is the authors' observation that there are several positive points associated with this method. Assertive discipline has alerted teachers and administrators to the need to formulate a uniform policy toward discipline and to communicate the school's philosophy, in terms of rules and resulting consequences, to parents. In utilizing this approach behavior expectations are clear. Rules are stated in a positive form. The entire school has the same disciplinary policy with administrative support. The rules apply to all the pupils. The method works as long as the teacher observes the deviant behavior and enforces the rules. Thus, when deviant behavior does occur, there is a consistent delivery of punishment. The beginning teacher may initially feel comforted by a delivery system which assists her in taking control of her class.

However, the intervention strategy and philosophical attitude which assertive discipline espouses has made this particular model highly controversial and, in many ways, antithetical to a child development point of view. In some ways this particular model seems to offer a quick fix to solving discipline problems. As we have indicated in this book, however, there is no easy solution to discipline problems and classroom management. Understanding and changing behavior is a multi-faceted and complex endeavor. In contrast, the teacher using assertive discipline techniques remains the ultimate power figure with little opportunity for youngsters to build self-discipline. It has also been our observation that teachers who take this approach quite literally tend to assume an adversarial position toward their pupils. Hitz (1988), has suggested that assertive discipline assumes children scheme and plot against teachers in some attempt to thwart the teaching/learning process. He further states (1988, p. 25), "...it appears that the method forces desirable behavior through power assertion rather than developing responsible behavior in children by rooting it in ethical purposes. Through assertive discipline children learn only that behavior is good because it is rewarded or bad because it is punished." Kamii (1984) points out that rewards and punishments should not be the principal method used in working with children since it prevents children from developing autonomy and a higher sense of moral development.

In terms of discipline, we feel the ultimate goal of education, both at home and school, is to help children develop their own internal control mechanisms which will enable them to make meaningful choices. Further, educators should help children assume responsibility, and accept the ultimate consequence of their decisions. In schools which use assertive discipline we have observed that teachers who employ the method but temper it with their own knowledge of learning theory and child development tend to have fewer discipline problems and a more positive attitude toward children.

For a more thorough discussion of the pros and cons of assertive discipline, the reader is referred to Gartrell (1987), Canter (1988), and Hitz (1988). Later, in Chapter Seven we will discuss our own philosophy concerning internal and external discipline and present the salient attributes of a "Discipline and Classroom Management Syndrome."

As we mentioned earlier, reinforcement strategies are not the ultimate solution. Making contracts and providing token, activity, and social reinforcement will not solve all behavior problems. Each child is unique and learning can occur via other methods. This book will explore these alternate methods of learning and their effect on the ways children behave. In the next section of this chapter we will discover that children can learn strategies of behaving through observation.

Modeling Behavior

For years people have noted that children often imitate their parents. It was probably these observations which lead to the old adage, "Like father, like son." We can observe modeling behavior in a two year old as he assumes the same physical stance as his father — shifting his feet, folding his arms, cocking his head in similar fashion. The authors remember watching a ten month old baby babbling in a strong husky voice for several minutes. Then the baby picked up a teddy bear. Holding the bear close to his body, the infant immediately changed his babbling pattern of speech to a quiet, cooing mode — actually duplicating some of the inflections of his mother.

Psychologists use the terms imitative or modeling behavior to describe these events. Freud pointed out the powerful role of parents in child rearing and noted that children often imitated their parents. Later John Watson, the behavioral psychologist, made similar observations. Since behavior was copied by youngsters, Watson offered some highly specific suggestions on ways in which parents should behave in rearing their children. In the 1950's Dollard and Miller theorized that parental nurturance was the guiding factor in children's imitation of parents. They postulated that, as parents satisfied the basic needs of children, they became reinforcing agents. Actually in the theory advanced by Dollard and Miller parents became "reinforcing attributes." Or — to use our earlier terminology — the parent is a "neutral cue." Thus, when parents are in the vicinity of a reinforcement, they, too, acquire drive value. As a result, children associate the parent with reduction of the drive and began to imitate this "nurturing adult." This imitative behavior becomes rewarding in and of itself.

However, children do not limit imitative behavior exclusively to their parents. Lewin and his students (Lippit and White, 1940) once did a study of group leadership. They used three types of leaders: democratic, autocratic and laissez-faire. They found that the type of leadership employed influenced the behavior of the entire group. Children began to imitate their leader and responded in ways appropriate to the climate the leader created. In the autocratic group, the children were often harsh with each other; in the democratic group, the children worked together in a spirit of cooperation. Interestingly, this modeling continued when the leader was not present in the room. The autocratic group became unruly and tyrannical when the leader was absent. The democratic group, on the other hand, continued much in the same spirit as when the leader was present. This research suggests some interesting questions for teachers. What type of leadership role does the teacher assume? How do children react to this role? What kind of classroom climate does the teacher create and how does this affect children.

Recently Bandura and his associates have carried on a number of studies which have extended our knowledge in the area of modeling. Their research is usually referred to as social learning theory. Based on this research the writers would make two general observations:

1. Children often model their behavior after the adult who teaches them.

Children do learn through imitation! This observation is very important to teachers and parents. It means that children closely observe adults and utilize their modes of behavior as a "model" for their own interactions. Please note the rule does not say: Children model the teacher's *good* behavior or *outstanding* behavior ... the statement refers to *all* behavior.

- On the days we holler: children learn.
- On the days we are unfair: children learn.
- On the days we tell children that we value individual differences; then treat all children alike: children learn.

A noisy teacher not only contributes to the noisy classroom; she often creates the situation. Thus, the child may ignore what is verbalized but imitate the actions of the teacher. The next time your classroom becomes unusually noisy — do not comment on the noise. Lower your own voice and speak clearly, but quietly. Usually, under these circumstances, the children will do likewise and the entire room will become quieter. The child views the teacher as a reinforcing property, per se, and imitates her behavior. Children will imitate the teacher's voice; her social overtures to others; her attitudes and even her mannerisms.

Several studies have found a high correlation between punitive parents and aggressiveness on the part of the child. Once a father said to the writers, "I don't know why George hits ... because every time he hits somebody I hit him!!" Obviously the child was modeling the behavior of his father. Studies also suggest that where parents lack sufficient self-control, their children often lack self-control.

2. Children model behavior they observe as being rewarded.

This is an important point for teachers. Earlier we observed that under certain conditions some negative reinforcers or acts of punishment could, in fact, be perceived as positive reinforcement.

Mary sees Adam hit Joey and take his car. Later she

observes Adam knock down some block towers and gleefully kick the blocks all over the room. She watches Adam take Hilda's place at the easel, forcing Hilda to go elsewhere. For all these wonderful feelings of power and dominance Mary also observes that the teacher merely says, "Adam, we share here." At storytime, after a series of misbehaviors the teacher says, "Adam, you must sit in my lap for while and calm down." In Mary's eyes, Adam has been beautifully rewarded for kicking, hitting and generally dominating others.

Bandura and his associates have found that children learn from a vicarious model, e.g., a character on TV or in the movies. Children model behavior which they see rewarded. Thus, even though the "bad guy" on television receives his punishment in the last 30 seconds of an episode, children may still imitate the earlier behaviors of the perpetrator. For example: The "bad guy" gets his way by hitting or killing; he obtains a new car by stealing; he avoids pain by lying; he makes fun of others by ridicule; he gets rich by cheating. Research suggests the child may learn more (be more influenced) by the large number of intermittent rewards and lose sight of the final punishment meted out just prior to the closing commercial.

The research on modeling does suggest that children indeed model their behavior after the adult who teaches them. Recently a teacher friend related the following observation to the authors. She said, "I have been teaching fourth grade in the same school for five years. There are two other fourth grade teachers and we all started in this school at the same time. This fall it finally dawned on me that classrooms do take on the personality of the teachers. Ms. Davis is a quiet calm teacher. She is rather strict and her classes are always the quietist of the three of us. Ms. Redmond is noisy and rather frenetic. Her class is always the loudest and the children always seem to be at 'loose ends.' She screams at them and they scream back. And, you know, in spite of the different children each year, it is amazing how the general Gestalt remains the same."

Learning Objectives for Chapter Three:

After reading Chapter Three, "How children learn," the reader should be able to:

1. Have an overview of the ways in which learning occurs.
2. Understand the role of drives in motivating behavior.
3. List ways to effect behavior change.
4. Discuss the importance of timing in discipline.
5. Given a problem in discipline, the reader should be able to:
   a. design strategies to maintain desirable behavior.
   b. decide the behavior to be changed and set attainable goals.
6. Discuss the importance of the teacher as a model and the effect of modeling behavior in discipline.
7. Discuss the role of reward and punishment and how it effects behavior change.
8. Define the following terms:

   drive   operant conditioning
   social drive   classical conditioning
   modeling   token reinforcement

Chapter Four

Recent Research Designs
That Really Help Teachers

In the past two decades there has been a large body of research in the area of discipline and classroom management. If you are a researcher in the behavioral sciences, the new knowledge in this area seems to border on the spectacular. There are several hundred studies related to school and teacher effectiveness, to types of discipline strategies, and refinements in instructional theory. However, if you are a classroom teacher who must daily encounter twenty-five children in various stages of mental and physical maturity and from a wide variety of cultural backgrounds — then the advances in "practical" discipline will seem to border on the trivial. It is difficult to take a highly structured research design with a small sample of children from a specific cultural milieu and relate these findings in any practical fashion.

In this chapter we will examine several studies which we believe can provide teachers with some insight into the techniques they use to change the behavior of children.

While it is impossible to translate research results into every classroom setting, this chapter outlines some major findings which should provide the teacher with some ideas and suggestions.

A few years ago at The Merrill-Palmer Institute in Detroit, Sigel and his associates did several studies on discipline. About the same time, at nearby Wayne State University, Kounin and his colleagues were conducting studies in the same general area. However, each group approached the subject matter from different vantage points — yet both have several practical implications for the teacher.

The Sigel Paradigm

Sigel and his associates became interested in the type of techniques a teacher used to influence the behavior of a child. They found the teacher had, in her repertoire, a number of influence techniques (IT) available to her at any given moment. These researchers studied the type of

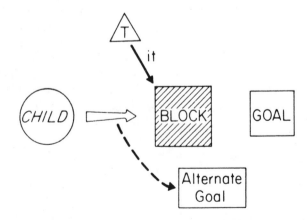

Figure 4.1

influence techniques used by teachers and their subsequent effectiveness on the child. (NOTE: We will refer to the child who receives the IT as the "target child." Thus, these researchers studied the types of IT used by teachers and their subsequent effectiveness on the target child. The Sigel paradigm is presented in Figure 4.1.

To explain this design, let us use an example: Johnny is headed toward a doll which is currently being used by Fan. The teacher, indicated by the triangle, determines that Johnny's behavior is unacceptable and decides to use an IT. In our example the teacher would say, "Johnny, Fan is playing with that doll. Here is a doll you may play with. Johnny accepts the proffered doll (the alternate goal). Utilizing this design, Sigel's group made several interesting observations which are helpful to the teacher.

1. If the influence technique is clear, the child is more likely to comply with the teacher's IT.

This observation appears to be so simple. That is, if the teacher clearly states a rule − or a reason − there is a greater likelihood that the child will positively respond to the teacher's wishes. While teachers and parents recognize this observation, it is amazing how often it is ignored. Generally adults use desist techniques which do not clarify rules or standards − nor do they provide any corrective help or information. In most cases the adult is remarkably unclear and shouts, "Quit" or "Stop that" or "That's enough!" After presenting unclear directions or fuzzy reasons, the adult then expects the child to somehow miraculously comply. Interestingly, most studies dealing with discipline show that the teacher more often focuses on stopping deviant behavior than she does on showing the child acceptable alternatives.

2. If the influence technique is consistent, the child is more likely to comply.

In Chapter Three, the importance of consistency was discussed as a major factor in reinforcement. In his research, Sigel also found this element of consistency to be extremely important. Quite simply stated, learning is much easier when the learning conditions remain constant. If children are to learn rules of behaving, the teacher must be consistent. Unfortunately, when the teacher is inconsistent, the net result is that the child begins to test the teacher — to discover the outer limits of the rules or to test the teacher's patience.

The following observation from a first grade setting illustrates inconsistent behavior on the part of the teacher: Ms. Roberts is with the Bluebirds reading group. Chuck and Lane are doing seatwork. Chuck says something to Lane.

Ms. Roberts: "Alright boys — stop." (The boys ignore Ms. Roberts and continue to talk...two minutes pass.)

Ms. Roberts: "Boys, shhh!"

The boys disregard the teacher's comments and continue to talk. One of the Bluebirds (Etta) says, "Ms. Roberts, I can't hear."

Ms. Roberts (Loud voice): "Alright, boys!!!" The boys continue to talk.

Ms. Roberts (Loud voice): "Chuck, if you and Lane do not stop, I am going to separate you."

The boys stop talking. They are quiet for nearly a minute and then commence talking again.

Ms. Roberts (Looks at boys, frowns): "Don't forget. I warned you."

Etta: "Ms. Roberts, I can't hear."

Ms. Roberts: "Just ignore them, Etta; they will get quiet in a minute."

In our example it is quite clear that Chuck and Lane have learned that the teacher does not carry out her admonitions. Therefore, they have learned to ignore her statements. We can observe similar inconsistent behavior on the part of the mother of a three year old.

C: "Mother can I go outside?"
M: "No, not now." (Mother is busy in the kitchen.)

C:"Mother, Please - Please, let me go out!"

M: "No, hush, I am busy."

C: (Pulls on mother's skirt) "Please! Please! Pretty please!!"

M: (Somewhat exasperated) "Will you be quiet! I am trying to cook...You are not going outside!!...and that is final!"

C: (Whining) "I want to play. I want to go out!!"

M: (Shakes head)

C: (Hits mother on leg) "Out!!"

M: "In a few minutes you can go out. Now, hush!"

C: (Hits mother on leg) "Out!! Out!!"

M: (Ignores hitting; continues working)

C: (Whining and stamping feet) "I want to go out now! Pretty please with sugar on it!"

M: "Well, since you said it nicely, I guess you can go out."

The child in our example has learned quite well. Mother's inconsistency has taught the child that if he is persistent for a long period of time, the rules will change.

3. If the influence technique offers the child an alternative, the child is more likely to comply.

Several years ago we conducted an informal study with a group of trained teachers and confirmed Sigel's observation. Teachers who offered child alternative solutions — or who redirected children to alternate goals — were more successful in terms of influencing behavior.   Unfortunately, we observed that teachers usually appeared too busy or too preoccupied to offer alternative approaches. Children were told that some action was prohibited — but were not provided any avenues toward acceptable behavior. (Please note that the teachers paid dearly for these transgressions — since we found they were less successful in terms of behavior management.)   Some examples may be useful:

Instead of: "Leave Mary's doll alone!"

Try: " There (point) is a doll you can play with."

Instead of: "Stop that!"
    Try: "I wonder if you could find another way to ... "

Instead of: "Don't throw those blocks ..."
    Try: "Let's get the bean bags and ... "

4. If the influence technique informs the child of future consequences, the child is more likely to comply.

Another influence technique, similar in character to an alternate goal, is to provide children with a warning. In this way youngsters are prepared for some future action or consequence. Most teachers have learned that children are more likely to comply with a suggestion, if they are advised of the action beforehand. Some examples will illustrate this point:

Instead of: "Marty, we are going outside."
    Try: "Marty, in five minutes it will be time to go outside.'

Instead of: "Michelle, pick up those blocks!"
    Try: "Michelle, when you finish building, remember to pick up the blocks."

In essence the warning provides the child with a psychological "set" (or predisposition) of a future consequence or action which will be taken. It is important to remember that once the "set" has been given, the teacher should follow thorough with the stated action at the appropriate time.

5. If the influence technique "reflects feelings," the child may respond in kind.

A commonly used control technique is to reflect the child's feelings. While this strategy may convey empathy to the child, discipline studies suggest that this approach may also have unusual repercussions. In observing the child's reactions to reflective influence techniques, it was observed that the child often became more upset. For example, when

80

the teacher used statements like, "You really are angry, aren't you?" or "I understand that you feel like hitting." It was observed that children often continued to hit or became even more angry than before.

Such observations suggest that the adult should carefully choose situations in which reflective techniques would be appropriate. It is quite possible that reflective techniques may actually contribute to the disturbance rather than having a calming effect.

6. The intensity of an influence technique has little relation to compliance.

Some teachers and parents feel that loud or rough talking will aid in compliance. The earlier example of Ms. Roberts illustrates that intensity has little relationship to the effectiveness of the IT. Sigel's associates found that of all the influence techniques available to the adult, "sheer power" was the least effective technique available to gain compliance.

In their study, they reported that "sheer power" was effective only about fifty percent of the time. Thus, if Sigel is correct, consider the following example:

Teacher: "Okay, Rene, I am really mad ... You cannot do that!! You will not hit!! I really mean you will stay right here ... You absolutely cannot hit Stephanie!"

Given the example above ... and, if the research finding is valid, about fifty percent of the time the child will still misbehave. Thus, in this instance, the chances are quite good that Rene will hit Stephanie — in spite of the teacher's use of a "sheer power" technique and absolute authority.

7. If the influence technique provides a "cushion," the child is more likely to comply.

81

The term, cushion, is used to describe a means by which the IT can be softened or made more palatable. Research shows that when the teacher employs a cushion, her chances of success dramatically improve. Even if she employs sheer power, her chances will be greater if she adds a cushion. Unfortunately, research also shows that most teachers do not utilize this technique. Osborn (1962) found eighty-nine percent of the time teachers employed a desist technique without any cushion. Some examples of influence techniques coupled with a cushion are presented below:

Instead of: "Everybody clean up!"
   Try: "In three minutes we will have to stop and clean up." (Here the IT is coupled with a "warning cushion.")

Instead of: "Leave that drill alone!"
   Try: "Jerri, the drill can be dangerous. Please wait until I can help you. (IT cushioned with reasoning.)

Instead of: "This is Abbey's puzzle."
   Try: "Burt, Abbey is playing with that puzzle. You may work with one of these." (IT cushioned with an alternative.)

Instead of: "Shut your mouth!"
   Try: "Noreen, you must be quiet now. After Simon speaks, you may have your turn. (In this last illustration the "sheer power" IT has been softened in volume and intent. Nevertheless the IT remains clear and definite and yet offers the child an avenue for appropriate behavior.)

The Kounin Paradigm

Kounin and his associates became interested in the "ripple effect" of discipline. The ripple effect is the effect a control technique exerts — not on the target child — but on the other children in the classroom as the technique "ripples out" from the target child. The Kounin paradigm is shown in Figure 4.2

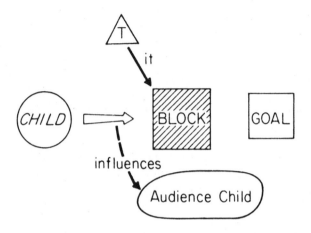

Figure 4.2

The following example may help to clarify the Kounin paradigm: Brenda is using counting blocks in math. She knocks the blocks on the floor. The teacher admonishes Brenda for her carelessness. In the Kounin research, the following questions would be raised. In correcting Brenda, what effect does the IT have on the children (the audience) sitting nearby? Does the type of technique employed make any difference to the audience child? Does the intensity of the IT have any effect on the audience?

The researchers found that the type of technique not only had an effect on the target child – it had an effect on the audience child as well. In other words, discipline does have a ripple effect. Children in the classroom learn by observing the discipline meted out to others. Kounin's associates report several significant findings which have meaning for teachers.

1. When the influence technique is clear, the audience children respond with increased conformance.

This finding is quite similar to Sigel's results with the target child. Kounin also found that when the control technique lacked clarity, the audience children responded with more non-conformity. This suggestion seems so obvious. If the teacher is clear in meting out her discipline, there is a greater likelihood that both the target child and the audience will improve in conformity. However, Ofchus (1980) found that 92 percent of the time teachers gave no reason why misbehavior was bad. In 96 percent of the cases the teacher did not clarify rules or group standards. Ofchus found that, in most instances, the teacher provided no clarity and little information beyond, "I will punish you in some fashion." We would suggest the following:

Instead of "Shh! Shh!"
Try: "Donna would you please speak softly so you won't disturb the rest of the class."

Instead of: "Zanette, quit!"
Try: "Zanette, you cannot hit Eulene." (Please note: In this example the teacher would increase the effectiveness of her IT if she provided an alternative for the child.)

2. When an influence technique is firm, the audience children respond with increased conformance.

The authors' own observations would suggest that this finding applies to the target child as well as audience children. Firmness is an interesting ingredient in discipline. It carries a degree of comfort for the child in the sense that the child usually translates firmness into knowing. Whenever a teacher is firm, a noticeable degree of assuredness accompanies this technique. Usually children are aware of this quality and conform to the teacher's IT.

One of the most difficult tasks in teacher education is to teach students how to be firm in their discipline. Students sometimes lack the "courage of their convictions" and this uncertainty is reflected in a lack of firmness. Classroom management does require rules. While rules should ideally be derived from democratic discussion, there are instances where this method is clearly inappropriate. The teacher must make a decision and carry it out with clarity and firmness.

Beginning teachers usually reflect their uncertainty by their general demeanor and manner in which they handle a discipline problem. If a particular child is difficult to manage, a beginning teacher will "ignore" misbehavior and hope the situation will magically resolve itself. Unfortunately, both the target child and the audience children learn that the teacher vacillates and is uncertain. This lack of firmness leads children to test limits.

One can observe uncertainty in a teacher's voice. For example: "Judy, don't you think you should share your toys?" This statement lacks firmness and clarity and reflects the teacher's indecisiveness. The absence of a firm commitment actually invites non-compliance.

Instead of: "Mario, you really don't want to hit Annie, do you?"
Try: "Mario, I will not permit you to hit Annie."

Instead of: "Class don't you think we could all hear better if we just decided to get quiet?"
Try: "Before we continue, the class must get quiet." (Note: If only two or three children are talking, the teacher will improve her IT by addressing these children by name. For example: "Tanya, before we continue, I want you and Troyce Anne to quit talking."

3. When an influence technique is rough, the audience children become upset.

Kounin's term "rough control technique" is the equivalent of Sigel's "sheer power" technique. Interestingly, both researchers found that this technique actually did little in controlling behavior. As mentioned earlier, Sigel found "sheer power" to be effective only about fifty percent of the time.

Kounin found (1970, p.54), "When teachers stopped a misbehavior with roughness (anger and/or punitiveness, but mostly anger) the audience pupils reacted with more behavior disruption (overt signs of apprehension or anxiety, less involvement in the ongoing task) than when teachers desisted without roughness ... children with punitive teachers manifested more conflict about classroom behavior, were less concerned about school manners and more preoccupied with aggression ... One might point out that punitiveness related not only to misbehavior and desist events, but was a general teacher mode of behavior that was applied to other issues, such as making mistakes in work."

The problem of high intense control techniques has been beautifully summarized by Kounin and Gump (1977, p. 160): "Roughness did not lead to increased conformance and decreased nonconformance. Instead rough techniques were followed by an increase in behavior disruption. *Severe techniques did not make for 'better' behavior in the child. Severe techniques merely upset him.*"

Teacher Effectiveness Studies

Kounin also presented another significant finding based upon his research. He noted differences between teachers who were effective managers and teachers who possessed poor management skills. His findings showed that teachers who were effective managers often prevented disruptive behavior. That is, the teacher saw that a problem was imminent and took steps prior to a disruptive situation. We would concur with Kounin's findings. In our own classroom observations, it is often obvious that some teachers are more attuned to the total classroom and the various interactions which are taking place among students. This inability to be aware of the total classroom *Gestalt* is a common failing among student teachers. Many times a student teacher will focus her attention on a single child and/or event and be unable to "back off" and observe the entire class setting. In addition, effective management and teaching often depends on being able to "look ahead" and see that a problem is about to occur.

Following up on the Sigel and Kounin research, Brophy and Evertson (1976), observed nearly sixty Texas teachers over a period of two years. Like Kounin, they found that good teacher management skills facilitated learning and made the operation of the classroom an easier task. Kounin used the term, "with-it" (see Chapter Seven) to describe teachers who were effective classroom managers and who could demonstrate to pupils, "I do know what is going on!"

An interesting study by Emmer, Evertson, and Anderson (1980), illustrates the importance of "setting the stage." These researchers closely observed a number of elementary classrooms for an entire year. They found a significant relationship between effective classroom organization during the first few weeks of school and effective discipline throughout the remainder fo the year. During the early weeks of the fall term, the effective teachers monitored students closely and dealt with problems immediately. Like the earlier studies by Kounin and Sigel, these researchers found that when influence techniques were clear, consistent, and firm, the classroom ran more smoothly and without unusual disruption. They also found that better managers were more explicit about what constituted desirable behavior.

Anderson, et al, (1979) also report similar findings. In addition they point out that effective managers taught going-to-school skills and provided practice for their pupils. Effective teachers did not ignore deviant behavior when it occurred. Rather these teachers gave immediate feedback, informed students when they were misbehaving, and provided them with corrective information.

In summary, the results of effective teacher studies show that good teacher managers are able to make clear to students what constitutes appropriate and/or deviant behavior. They are more consistent in managing behavior and quickly react with dispatch when they observe deviant behavior. Effective teachers are also more efficient managers in that they waste less time and are engaged in more on-task behavior. Early in the year they establish rules and routines for their class. In addition, they take sufficient time to teach their students these procedures so that they understand teacher expectations. Obviously, a vital part of effective teaching is to be able to make the rules clear and to be able to give directions and communicate effectively with the students.

Learning Styles & Cognitive Monitoring

Recent research in the area of learning styles offers suggestions to teachers in terms of discipline and classroom management. These studies (Dunn & Dunn, 1978), suggest that children are generally less disruptive when teachers can adapt their instruction to the child's "style of learning." As Chapter One in this text points out, the more the teacher knows about an individual learner, the better she will be able to understand his behavior and thus be able to help the youngster.

Studies in this area (Joyce & Weil, 1980; Dunn, 1983), suggest that children will learn more effectively when teachers help them utilize the styles or methods of learning which are most productive for them. Some children appear to learn more effectively by listening to material; others by seeing the subject matter content. The effective teacher determines ways to "match" the child with the appropriate style or styles of learning and structures a creative, enriched learning environment.

Another area of productive research is termed, "cognitive monitoring." It is also referred to as CBM — cognitive behavior management, (Meichenbaum, 1977). This technique involves several self-control skills. One technique involves the use of teacher modeling and verbal self-instruction. Rather than merely "telling children," the teacher demonstrates the technique which includes self-instruction, self-monitoring, and self-reinforcement. This technique involves cognitive self-instructional strategies to guide and control behaviors in a manner similar to the acquisition of self-regulating behaviors (speech for oneself) as postulated by Vygotsky (1934). Meichenbaum utilizes five steps with the CBM technique: 1) The teacher models a task while talking out loud. 2) The child does the task under teacher instruction. 3) The child performs the task while saying the instructions out loud. 4) The child whispers the material while actually doing the task. 5) The child can accomplish the task without outside help and utilizes private speech (talking to himself). Some studies in this area suggest that significant changes in behavior can result when youngsters internalize the *raison d'etre* for their behavior and then reinforce themselves for that behavior.

Manning (1988), studied 30 first grade and 25 third grade children who were exhibiting inappropriate classroom behaviors. The children were placed in two groups. The experimental group received CBM in eight training sessions over a period of four weeks. In these sessions, Manning used a cueing technique which encouraged students to remind themselves to bring their own behavior under their own control. Following the training, students in the experimental group (both 1st & 3rd graders), received higher on-time-on-task ratings and took more personal responsibility for their actions than did the control youngsters. In Chapter Seven some practical suggestions are presented on ways to use the cueing method for helping in classroom self-control.

Glasser's Reality Therapy

In his research, Glasser (1969,1977), has modified certain psychiatric principles which may be useful to teachers as an approach for students who persist in engaging in deviant behavior. Glasser's theory, called Reality Therapy, is a psychodynamic model. However, unlike other psychodynamic theories which are described in Chapter One, Glasser's theory is ahistorical; that is, it does not ask the teacher to examine antecedent conditions or the child's past experiences. Glasser believes that the historical approach and analyzing a person's inner conflicts is generally inefficient. Glasser believes that every person is capable of being rational and responsible. The central tenants of his theory include: individuals must live in a world with others in such a way as to not infringe on the rights of others; a person is responsible for his own actions and must bear the consequences for these actions; and, finally, an individual must make a commitment to act responsibly toward others.

In his book, *Schools without failure,* Glasser (1969) states that it is the responsibility of the teacher to provide a classroom of relevant activities which motivate students to want to succeed. He suggests that teachers and students should jointly agree on the rules of the classroom. Students agree to abide by these rules and are then held responsible for their own behavior. According to Glasser, teachers should maintain a positive problem solving approach and administer the rules in a fair and just manner.

In his article, "Ten steps to good discipline," Glasser (1977) offers some suggestions for students who continue to engage in deviant behavior. The ten steps include: Selecting a student for concentrated attention and analyzing discipline techniques which are effective. The teacher should resolve to stop using techniques which prove ineffective. The teacher should concentrate on improving personal relationships with the student and provide more attention and encouragement. In addition, the teacher should have a conference with the pupil and focus attention on the deviant behavior. The student is asked to discuss and describe his behavior. Then, a plan is devised to solve the inappropriate behavior and to obtain the student's commitment to abide by the agreement. The student also agrees that the plan will be enforced by the teacher.

If the problem behavior persists, Glasser suggests isolating the student or using time out procedures. During the period of isolation the student is expected to focus on the problem and devise a plan to help resolve the problem. If the misbehavior persists, Glasser proposes an in-school suspension. The student must then deal with the principal or someone other than the teacher. If the in-school suspension is unsuccessful, the youngster is expelled from school for one day. If the student is still unable to respond to the previous steps, Glasser suggests he be removed from school and referred to another agency.

Research Reviews

In this chapter we have presented highlights of research studies which we believe are particularly helpful to the teacher and which can be translated into classroom practice. As we mentioned at the beginning of this chapter, the past twenty years has seen a large body of research in discipline and classroom management. For the reader who wishes more information, the following references are suggested.

Hoffman (1970), an associate of Sigel's, presents an excellent review of earlier studies related to influence techniques. Duke (1982) edited a book for ASCD which provides an extensive bibliography plus several articles on classroom management and teacher effectiveness. The 1979 NSSE Yearbook is devoted to classroom management and contains an excellent bibliography. There are three chapters in volume 4 of the *Handbook of Child Psychology* (Mussen, 1983) which readers will find particularly helpful. Minuchin's chapter on the school as a context for social development; Radke-Yarrow's chapter on children's prosocial behavior; and Parke and Slaby's chapter on the development of aggression. Each chapter contains many references. Honig (1985a;1985b) traces the development of compliance from birth through the preschool years and cites a number of studies which show the importance of parenting practices. These studies clearly show that the quality of child rearing is closely related to the child's competence, compliance, flexibility in problem solving and resourceful ability to seek adult assistance.

Learning Objectives for Chapter Four:

After reading Chapter Four, "Recent research designs that really help teachers," the reader should be able to:

1. Identify influence (discipline) techniques which will be most successful in a classroom setting.
2. Differentiate between firmness and roughness in administering discipline.
3. Differentiate between a power technique and a cushion technique and discuss the relative value of the technique chosen.
4. Compare techniques with clarity and consistency and discuss the relative value of the techniques chosen.
5. Identify the research paradigms utilized in the chapter and compare ways in which the designs are alike and different.
6. Cite differences in teacher effectiveness and the significance of different learning styles in children.
7. Discuss Meichenbaum's five steps utilizing the CBM technique.
8. Discuss Reality Therapy. What is Glasser's philosophy about students? What are some strengths and weaknesses of this model?

Chapter Five

Drugs: A Special Problem

The problem of drugs has become pervasive in American Society. Initially a problem in big city ghettos, drugs can be found in small cities and towns. In a 1989 survey of 100 rural Georgia counties, the *Atlanta Journal* reported that 83% of the sheriffs in those counties stated that crack was a significant law-enforcement problem. For example, in one county the local sheriff reported that of the 42 inmates currently in jail; 19 were there for crimes related to crack. Kumpfer (1987) reports that the direct and indirect cost of alcohol and drug abuse to the average American citizen is between $850 to $1,000 yearly. Of course, alcohol and drug users spend much more to support their own addiction. By way of comparison, the federal government and local education agencies, will spend less than $1.85 per child in order to educate youngsters about drugs and drug prevention.

Drugs are everywhere. Many of the drugs we use are perfectly legal; they are used daily and can serve many good purposes. Some drugs have a medicinal value and may help the individual for whom they were prescribed. Nose drops, eye drops and drugs like tobacco, aspirin, coffee, and alcohol may be seen as reasonably harmless. Unfortunately, a large number of persons misuse these and a host of other drugs.

Until recently drugs were relatively unknown in the public schools. In the 1940's and 1950's, a youngster might smoke a cigarette in the school rest room — or a high school student might "sneak" a half-pint of gin into the punch bowl of the junior-senior prom. Most students were as innocent as the youngsters depicted on the television program, "Webster."

Unfortunately events in the late 1960's and early 1970's caused changes in our attitudes and behavior. In the process the children of America lost their innocence. College kids were encouraged to "drop out" and "turn on." LSD, alcohol, marijuana, and angel dust became common on the college scene. Fraternities began to have "fruit salad" parties where participants all brought a variety of pills and made a "salad" which was guaranteed to give you a "high" or make you sick.

Today there is an epidemic among children in the United States and in other parts of the world. Like the plagues of the Middle Ages, this epidemic may wipe out nearly a total generation. However, this epidemic will not kill — rather it will harm our children psychologically by killing ambition and the desire to succeed. It will dull their conscious awareness and lull them into a false feeling of well-being. For many children it will cause them to commit burglaries and thefts and become involved in illicit sex. This epidemic will also harm our children physically by causing brain damage, liver and lung ailments. When they become adults their own children may be born with birth defects as a result of drugs.

Incidence of Drug Abuse

Many teachers and parents have failed to realize the extent of the drug problem. Recently the authors were giving a lecture in a small community in one of our southeastern states. In casual conversation several teachers and parents commented, "We really do not have a drug problem in our little city. We have a few high school kids who get drunk ... and we may have some alcohol abuse ... but very few of our students ever see marijuana, crack, or any of the hard drugs."

The next day we interviewed several high school students in that same community. The following comments are excerpted from that interview:

I don't see how some of our parents and teachers can be so stupid! We have drugs everywhere. I can get on the telephone and have pot delivered here in fifteen minutes ... We used to smoke pot on the school bus, but the driver recognized the smell and made us stop. Now we just roll joints on the bus ... some kids who get on the bus are already stoned out of their gourds. The most common place to buy drugs in in the bathroom at school. Actually I am pretty lucky ... two of my girl friends are dealers. In fact, one of the richest kids in town is a dealer; his dad is president of the local bank. He makes about four hundred bucks a week selling crack and marijuana. A couple of the guys from the "poor" neighborhood have really cool cars— they got the cars from the money they made selling drugs. Parents are really dumb! If they even thought about this, they would *know* that these guys didn't have any way of owning nice automobiles. The only way you can have that kind of "big" money is from dealing in drugs. Almost everybody is into alcohol, pot, or crack. If you don't smoke grass, there really isn't anything else to do at a party ... you would just be sitting around while everybody else gets high. There is a lot of peer pressure to participate. Teachers are really stupid too! In my one o'clock class the teacher is always talking about how nice the class is ... it should be!! Half of the class is high on grass!

We asked these students the extent of drug usage in their school. They replied, "At least sixty to seventy percent of the kids smoke pot, use crack, or take something like Valium ... but almost everybody has tried something, even if they don't use the stuff regularly."

Teachers must recognize that drugs are rapidly becoming a "way of life" for many students in the middle and high school. Elementary school teachers must be alerted to the fact that smoking, drinking and marijuana use are occurring more frequently in the early grades. (See Figures 5.1 and 5.2)

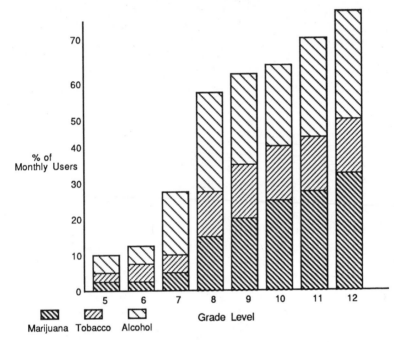

Incidence of Marijuana, Tobacco, & Alcohol by Grade Level
The Gateway Drugs

Figure 5.1

Percentage of 13 year olds who used Marijuana
1953-1982

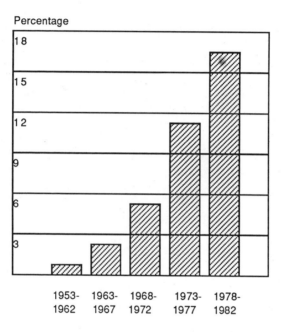

Figure 5.2

Children as young as nine and ten years of age are beginning to experiment with drugs. Also, it is sad to report that we have found several cases in which parents have turned their children on to drugs. There have been several instances where young mothers have blown marijuana smoke into the mouths of their infant children in an effort to get the babies "high" so they would stop crying. Recently one of our former graduates, a kindergarten teacher, told us about one of her students. It seems that the mother was giving the child a joint each morning in order to "calm the child down." Remember this is a five year old youngster!

Addiction has been called the "American disease." One prominent official in the National Institute of Drug Abuse stated, "This country appears to be particularly vulnerable to the drug craze. At one end of the economic spectrum the affluent group abuses drugs and will avail itself of any thrill which can be purchased — and on the other end is the poverty stricken element of society where social alienation and drug abuse is a way of life." Rep. Lester Wolff (D., N.Y.), chairman of the Select Committee on Narcotics Abuse and Control, stated: "The United States is the most pervasive drug-abusing nation in history." The U.S. has the highest rate of teenage drug use of any industrialized nation. The drug problem in this country is twelve times greater than Japan; seven times greater than Germany.

The Institute for Social Research and the Wolff committee provide the following statistics:

• Between 4 and 5 million kids between the ages of 11 to 17 are smoking pot on a reasonably regular basis.

• Sixty-one percent of high school seniors have used drugs. Forty-one percent of 1985 seniors reported using marijuana in their senior year. Thirty-six percent said they had used it at least once the previous month.

• Eleven percent of all high school students (1 student in 9) are smoking pot on a *daily* basis. High school users smoke about 3 1/2 joints per day.

• Pot smoking is now common among middle school students. Pot smoking is on the increase among 8 to 12 year olds.

• In 1962, marijuana use among 13 year olds was virtually nonexistent. Today about one in six 13 year olds have used marijuana.

• Thirteen percent of high school seniors indicated that they used cocaine in the past year. This is more than double the number of users in 1975.

The National Institute on Drug Abuse (NIDA) furnishes the following statistics:

• Before they graduate from high school about 80% of all kids will have smoked marijuana.

• 70% of the high school kids who smoke pot, admit to driving while they are "high" on marijuana. 75% of the high school children who drink alcohol, admit to driving while mildly intoxicated.

• 68% of all persons between the ages of 18 to 25 have used pot.

• There are 4,000,000 problem drinkers in the 16-25 year old group. The average age of beginning alcohol use is 12 years; some students report starting as early as 8-10 years of age.

• By the time they graduate from high school, nearly 75% of all students will have used alcohol.

• Alcohol abuse is involved in about 80% of domestic violence, 70% of child sexual abuse cases, and 40% of family court actions.

• 9,000 teenagers are killed in alcohol related auto accidents. An additional 40,000 teens are injured every year in automobiles where the cause is DUI.

Of course, the increased use of alcohol and drugs is reflected in every segment of our society. A Gallup Poll (1977) reported that only four percent (4%) of the American population used marijuana in 1969. By 1973, marijuana use had climbed to 12%. By 1977, there had been a 100% increase with 24% of the American population reporting that they used marijuana. A NIDA report shows that alcohol and drug abuse is the third leading cause of illness in the United States. Reports also indicate that nearly 40% of emergency admissions to hospitals are related to substance abuse. Estimates on alcohol and drug abuse in the work force include:

- Industrial workers — 18%
- Office workers — 21%
- Medical professions — 26%
- Sports professions — 31%
- Entertainment industry — 40%

The Wolff committee reported that a study in California found that children usually begin to experiment with drugs in the fifth grade and some children reported using drugs as early as the second and third grade.

Robert DuPont, former director of NIDA stated: "In all of history no young people have ever used drugs regularly on a mass scale. Therefore, our youngsters are, in effect, making themselves guinea pigs in a tragic national experiment. Thus far, our research clearly suggests that we will see horrendous results."

The Effect of Drugs on Learning and The School Climate

Among teenagers there is a "myth" that some drugs will enhance learning, improve one's memory, and increase IQ. Often drugs like "uppers" will be used by students to help them remain awake and stay up for long "cramming" sessions. Such cramming sessions are very common in colleges just prior to mid-terms and finals. However, short term "cramming" sessions result in learning which is short-lived. Most learning which occurs as a result of cramming is quickly forgotten.

Drugs can destroy self-discipline and the original motivation for learning. Continued use of drugs is destructive to learning and finally results in a decline in academic performance. Parents and teachers may notice a change in student behavior as a result of using drugs. Often children who were good students will do an "about face" and become disinterested in school. Studies have indicated that students using marijuana are twice as likely to average Ds and Fs as other students.

There is a high correlation between truancy and school dropouts. Studies show that students who are using drugs are more likely to skip classes and/or school. In a study conducted in a large Pennsylvania city, there was a statistically significant relationship between frequent drug users and high school dropouts. Four out of five dropouts in this study were also heavy drug users.

Drug use and abuse can drastically affect the school's physical environment as well as the learning climate. In schools where drug use is heavy, children are often afraid to use the rest room facilities because bathrooms have become the most common meeting place for drug transactions. Student drug pushers may have knives or other weapons. It is not uncommon for a drug pusher to carry four or five hundred dollars in cash. This situation often leads to robbery, fighting, class disorder, and the destruction of school property.

Types of Abused Drugs

There are several ways in which one can group the most commonly abused drugs. For our purposes we have divided the drugs into four major groupings. These are: depressants, stimulants, psychedelics, and psychotropics.

Depressants can cause both chemical and/or psychological dependence. Continued use will result in drug tolerance and the need for a larger dose. Stopping the drug after prolonged use can cause severe withdrawal including nerv-

101

ousness, insomnia, anxiety and even death. Depressants are muscle relaxants and small amounts will have a calming effect. Larger doses will produce slurred speech, uncertain gait, and altered perception. An overdose can cause respiratory problems and even coma or death. Any combination of depressants (or coupled with alcohol) can be extremely dangerous.

Some writers have a separate category for narcotics. However, we have included narcotics under this grouping since they are actually depressants. Narcotics initially produce a feeling of euphoria that is often followed by lack of coordination, drowsiness and nausea. The user may experience severe depression following use and a intense desire for more of the drug. Users have constricted pupils, watery eyes. An overdose will produce slow and shallow breathing, convulsions, coma, and death. Narcotics are both physically and psychologically addictive and withdrawal can be severe.

Drug Type: Depressants

Drug Type	Examples
Barbituates	Phenobarbital, Nembutal, Seconal
Mild Tranquilizers	Librium, Valium, Miltown, Equanil, Serax
Methaqualone	Quaaludes, Ludes
Alcohol	Beer, wine, wine coolers, hard liquor
Inhalants	Aerosols, Nitrous Oxide, Butyl Nitrite (Rush), Hydrocarbons (solvents, glue)
Narcotics	Heroin, Methadone, Codeine, Morphine, Demoral, Opium

Psychedelic drugs include cannabis and the hallucinogens. Cannabis is, of course, the scientific name for mari-

forms of cannabis have negative physical and mental effects. It can be habit forming and is commonly called the "gateway" drug. Marijuana, called pot, grass, weed, Mary Jane, and Acapulco Gold, can produce forms of paranoia and other psychotic symptoms. It can cause insomnia, impair memory, motor coordination, alter a sense of time, and tasks requiring concentration. Smoking marijuana can cause damage to the lungs and and pulmonary system.

Hallucinogens interrupt the function of the neocortex — the brain area which controls the intellect and certain instincts. Since, these drugs block pain receptors, a user may inflict serious self-injury. An overdose can produce heart and lung failure, coma, and convulsions. Extended use may cause memory and speech problems. Illusions and halluci-nations are quite common under regular use. One of the problems with the hallucinogens is that a person may experience a delayed effect or a flashback after stopping drug use.

Drug Type: Psychedelics

Drug Type	Examples
Cannabis	Marijuana, Hash Oil, Hashish
Hallucinogens	LSD, PCP (Angel Dust), Mescaline

Stimulants include a wide variety of drugs. They can cause increase heart and respiratory rate and cause elevated blood pressure. One of the most notable symptoms for many drugs in this category are dilated pupils. Users can experience headaches, blurred vision, insomnia, dizziness, restless-ness, and irritability. A well-known methylphenidate in this category is Ritalin. This drug is in common use with children diagnosed as having minimal brain dysfunction or other psychological, educational, or social disorders. High use over a long period of time will lead to chemical dependence. The most common problems of overuse of this drug can include loss of appetite, stomach pains, insomnia and abnormal heart rhythms.

The most widely abused substances in this category are: caffeine, nicotine, and cocaine. Nicotine can cause cancer as well as heart and lung damage. Cocaine stimulates the central nervous system. Chronic use of cocaine (through snorting or sniffing) will cause damage to the nasal septum. Freebase, which involves the use of highly flammable solvents, can result in death or serious injury from fire or explosion. Cocaine is highly addictive, both psychologically and physically. Users report being "in love" or "enslaved" to cocaine. Freebase is extremely addictive. A relatively new drug of use is called crank. This is a methamphetamine and is usually made in home laboratories. The drug is a white powder and its effect is similar to crack (cocaine).

Drug Type: Stimulants

Drug Type	Examples
Caffeine	Coffee, cola drinks
Nicotine	Cigarettes, cigars
Cocaine	Cocaine, crack
Amphetamine	Dexedrine, Ferndex, Dexampex
Metthamphetamine	Crank
Other stimulants	Ritalin, Cylert, Preludin, Tepanil

Psychotropics include strong tranquilizers and anti-depressants. These drugs are usually prescribed for psychotic disorders and severe depression. These drugs have a sedative effect and induce drowsiness. In some persons, however, they can have the opposite effect and cause inability to sleep, abnormal heart rates, hallucinations and disorientation. In severe cases, delusions, convulsions, and death.

Drug Type: Psychotropics

Drug Type	Examples
Anti-depressants	Elavil, Amitrip, Emitrip
Strong tranquilizers	Compazine, Thorazine

A detailed chart showing types of drugs and their effects is available to educators, without cost, from the Drug Enforcement Administration, The Department of Justice, Washington, DC 20533. The title of the chart is "Controlled Substances: Uses and Effects." There is also an extensive description of drugs and their effects in the booklet, *Schools without drugs*, which is available from the U.S. Department of Education, Washington, DC 20202.

Why Children Use Drugs

Recent studies have addressed questions related to the onset of drug and alcohol abuse. (Kandel, 1975; Sherman et al, 1983; Johnson et al, 1986). Researchers have begun to focus on three "gateway" substances — tobacco, alcohol and marijuana. In most cases, youngsters use gateway drugs before "graduating" to hard drugs. Studies also suggest that gateway substances are not in general use, prior to the onset of adolescence. For example, Johnson has shown that use of these products is relatively rare among preadolescents. Johnson found that in the 5th grade the incidence of tobacco use was 5%; alcohol 10%; and marijuana 2%. As youngsters entered later grades the incidence on use of these substances increased. For example, Johnson found 19% (marijuana); 33% (tobacco); and 60% (alcohol) of the 9th graders in his study reported that they used these substances monthly.

Peer Pressure

Research shows that the greatest single cause for the initial use of drugs is pressure from the peer group. Probably the first big "test" in life outside the realm of the family is the pressure which is exerted by youngsters who are the same age or just slightly older. Youngsters can exert tremendous pressure by saying, "act grown up" and "everybody's doing it." In 1988, a survey conducted by *The Weekly Reader* found that the most important reason for smoking marijuana was to "fit in" with the peer group.

Even in the first grade the child is influenced by his peer group. While the impact is relatively small, it does have an effect on the child's attitudes and opinions. In the first grade, the child may learn "group words," "toilet language" and silly poems like, "No more classes, no more books, no more teacher's dirty looks." Peers do teach children to model after the rest of the group.

In the early grades, however, the peer group's influence is relatively mild. The child will turn to the teacher and the parent for guidance and receive "superego" strength from these adults. He will value and abide by adult counsel. Most children will say to their playmates, "I cannot do that because my mother would not like it." Or, "The teacher said that we should walk in line and not talk with our neighbor." In the early school years, children view adults as heroes and best friends. These adults represent ideals children would like to emulate.

About 11 or 12 years of age — and during the adolescent years, the desire to be liked and accepted by the peer group becomes of paramount importance. During this period the relative influence of the teacher and parent declines. Discipline techniques which were effective in the first, second and third grade will often backfire. Can you imagine a high school teacher saying, "I would like to see all my good citizens sit up straight and not talk to their neighbor!" In fact, some students will purposely go counter to the wishes of the teacher just to attain status in the peer group. Thus, if the teacher chastises a child — the youngster's status in the peer group may be increased.

Peer pressure in the pre-adolescent and adolescent years can often be more exacting and cruel than at any other time in life. The peer group can make a child's life seem almost unbearable. The fear of being rejected coupled with the desire to be liked can be overwhelming at times — particularly since the importance of the peer group takes on an extremely powerful role during this period.

Adolescence is a time of social-biological-psychological change. The child is undergoing tremendous physical changes within his body. In addition he is going from the world of childhood to the world of adulthood. Values are examined and questioned and the youngster begins to experiment with new ideas and new materials. In today's world, this experimentation can include driving an automobile at reckless speeds, testing authority in many areas, and taking drugs.

The earlier section on drug incidence showed that in many schools over 80% of all high school seniors have tried marijuana, tranquilizers, alcohol or other drugs. Some schools report the percentage is as high as 90-95%. In other words more high school seniors have experimented with drugs than youngsters who have not.

In our conversations with high school students many report that using crack, smoking grass or getting drunk is the "thing to do." Youngsters who have not tried drugs encounter tremendous peer pressure. One girl told us, "When I was in high school I did not have any friends who were not using grass. I seldom went to parties because there was so much pressure to get high. It was almost impossible to have friends if you didn't use drugs."

Other reasons for using drugs

In addition to peer pressure, we should recognize that there are other factors which may be involved in causing children to use drugs. One major factor in drug use among young people is that they view drugs as relatively harmless. There are several reasons for having this point of view. Children see their parents using tobacco and alcohol. They see their grandmother take Valium. Our society has viewed drugs as part of our normal life-style. In addition, in the 1960's, reports stated that marijuana was less harmful than cigarettes. LSD was supposed to give you amazing insights. PCP was supposed to give the user a pleasant high and reveal a lovely world. Cocaine was considered a safe "Yuppie" drug which was harmless and non-habit forming. Early medical research and government reports during that period were often vague and confusing. Today the data on drug abuse is much clearer. Unfortunately, many teachers are unaware of the latest findings and continue to view drugs as relatively harmless. This lack of knowledge is particularly true in terms of marijuana and cocaine use. The reader should study the effects of continued drug use as outlined in the section on abused drugs. In addition the reader is referred to the special drug bibliography at the end of the chapter.

One reason that drugs are viewed as harmless rests with the mass media and its impact on youngsters. Children in elementary and middle grades view television and movies as a powerful factor in their lives. In a recent survey these youngsters stated that next to the peer group — television and movies played the most influential role in their lives and had a decided impact on their behavior. Often these youngsters believed that the media view makes drugs and alcohol seem quite attractive. In many TV shows the super-heroes and MCs treat pot, crack, and other drugs in a casual manner. It is not unusual to hear guests on shows like "Saturday Night Live" and "The Johnny Carson Show" make light references to pot or cocaine use. A number of movies show early teens using marijuana or crack. Note: Within the past year, due in part to the concerns of the White House, movies have tended to place less emphasis on drug use by the protagonists. However, older movies continue to be shown on HBO and other TV channels. Even the movie, "Nine to Five" has a "funny" sequence involving the use of marijuana. Some comedians use jokes with double meanings one for the "straights," another for the drug users.

Popular music has many references to drugs, pot, getting drunk and getting high. For example, an old Beatle favorite, "Lucy in the Sky with Diamonds." The letters in the title refer to LSD. Popular rock and heavy metal groups make numerous references to drugs, satanic rituals, and explicit sex.

Many books and magazines glamorize the drug culture. They promise that drugs will provide great new insights, enhance lives, encourage creativity, and understanding. Magazines like "High Times," with a reader circulation of nearly five million, push the joys of drugs and drug use. Their motto is: "(This magazine) ... is about your favorite leisure activities pot, hash, coke, LSD and a host of other natural highs." Stores which sell drug paraphernalia (called "Head Shops") are open to children of all ages. Corner mini-markets with their cigarette papers, incense and clay pipes all suggest to youngsters that using drugs is okay.

Another reason for increased drug use is accessibility. Crack, crank, pot, and pills are readily available in most middle and high schools in America today. Grass can be obtained for less than one dollar and crack is available for less than ten dollars. As cocaine has become the "middle class drug of preference," the price on the street has actually lowered in the past eight years. Children we have interviewed state that the best place to obtain drugs is at school.

As adolescents show their independence from parental authority, they rebel in a variety of ways. For many years the use of tobacco and alcohol were considered "adult habits."

Adolescents often indulge in tobacco, beer, and wine to prove that they are mature. Drugs create a feeling of excitement and doing something "naughty." They give some children the sense of doing something dangerous like the old days when teenagers played "chicken." Even though youngsters may believe that some drugs are potentially dangerous, adolescents have a feeling that they will live forever. They have a real sense that, "I cannot be killed ... that happens to someone else ... other guys have 'bad trips' ... it won't happen to me."

Drugs are easy to use. Pills are easy to hide and can be swallowed quickly. Cocaine comes in white powder form and is usually sniffed or "snorted" through a straw and into the nose. Marijuana looks like small leaves, dried grass or oregano. Marijuana can be smoked as a cigarette or in a small pipe. Crack is sold in pieces which look like soap chips or small white pellets. Some crack looks like small bits of white gravel. Crack can be placed in a cigarette or in a pipe. Most drugs are easily disposable and the visible effects are gone after smoking, they can be consumed in school rest rooms or in a remote corner of the playground.

There is a very disturbing reason for drug use in the case of pre-teens. In many situations children 8-10 years of age are first introduced to drugs by an older brother or sister. There is a high correlation between early use by a child who has a sibling already on drugs. Another finding, perhaps the most unsettling, is that some drug addicted parents are turning their own children on to drugs.

We should mention one other major reason why children use drugs. Drugs provide the user with a variety of feelings — some drugs can make you feel drowsy; others can help you to be more alert ... you may feel like you are "taking off" or "floating" or like a blast of air is hitting you in the face (called a "rush"). Drugs can make you happy, sad, help you remember, help you forget, help you feel accepted, more social, avoid a painful experience. Some heavy users· of

110

cocaine have hallucinations that the "coke" is actually talking to them. Drugs can give you a feeling of self-assurance, daring and bravado.

Initially, many drugs *do* make you feel good. They give one a feeling of euphoria — they make you "temporarily" forget your troubles — your problems seem less or they seem to disappear altogether. When persons are "high" on drugs or alcohol, they usually feel happy and believe that they are in complete control. Crack can give a high for about five minutes but the euphoria is often followed by depression

It is easy to see how drugs have taken hold in our culture. They have become as common as mom and apple pie. If we are to help children face the drug issue we must understand their reasons for taking drugs. While the influence of the peer group is extremely strong, it does not mean that the adult world is powerless in its battle against drug use. Later in this chapter we will discuss some things the teacher can do to cope with the situation.

Drug Addiction

We know that if a person never takes a drink, ingests pills, smokes marijuana, or snorts cocaine — he or she will not become addicted to these substances. We also know that some persons will experiment with alcohol and drugs and never become chemically dependent. Unfortunately, however, a large percentage of individuals may develop an addiction after a very brief period of time. Some persons appear so "addictive prone" they are "hooked" after their first trial. The problem is very complex and there are a myriad of influences which impact on causes of addiction. Researchers have attempted to establish an "addictive model" or profile which would unequivocally designate a potential addict. To date, however, researchers have been unable to determine exactly why some persons become addicted to drugs and alcohol and others do not.

Researchers in this field have constructed two basic models: physical and psychological. According to the Prevention Research Institute, Lexington, Kentucky, every person has a certain level of risk for any given health problem. This level is determined by biological factors — either genetic or acquired. Thus, some individuals are biologically disposed toward chemical dependence. For example, research has shown that children of alcoholics are five times more likely to become alcoholics than children of non-alcoholic parents.

In the psychological model, an individual initially turns to alcohol or drugs for any number of social and/or personal reasons. A recent report by the National Research Council found that stress, anxiety, depression, a sense of social alienation, impulsivity, panic disorders, nonconformity, a general tolerance for deviance, and impulse gratification were factors which comprised the psychological model syndrome. As use of alcohol or drugs continues, the individual develops a "psychological" dependency. In many instances a chemical dependency will follow and exacerbate the problem.

Signs of Drug Use By Your Students

Usually the first and most common drug used by children is marijuana. Marijuana is referred to as the "gateway drug" since, in most cases, persons who use other drugs have started their drug career by smoking pot. Studies have shown that the greater a youngster's involvement with marijuana, the greater the likelihood that he or she will start to use more potent drugs in conjunction with marijuana.

In addition to marijuana, some children under twelve begin by sniffing glue or using inhalants such as: aerosols, gasoline, correction fluid, paint thinner, cleaning agents and butyl nitrite. (See the earlier section on drug abuse and Appendix D for effects of drug use.) While it is not always possible to determine if children are using drugs, there are a number of clues and symptoms which should alert the teacher to possible drug involvement.

• Listen to conversation. Be particularly alert to the conversation of your children. Quite often they will use drug terminology because it makes them feel "cool" or a more integral part of the drug culture. For example, if you hear one child ask another, "Can you do me a favor?" the child may be asking for a joint. This does not mean that if you hear a child say "pot," he is a user. However, the teacher should check further into the child's activities. (See Appendix E for a glossary of drug terms.)

• Examine notebooks. Often "drug phrases" are written on the covers of notebooks and in texts, scrapbooks and yearbooks. Statements are often written like, "Power through Pot," "Let's mow the grass," "Fruit salad isn't just for fruits."

• Look for cigarette papers. We mentioned earlier that many adults feel that marijuana and other drugs are "harmless." Notice how many "nice" mom and pop stores and mini-markets sell cigarette papers. This is particularly true in neighborhood stores near schools and in the service stations which have "game rooms."

• Look for plastic or cellophane "baggies." These are used to hold marijuana. Look for other drug paraphernalia — "coke" spoons, small mirrors, pipes or containers to hide pot. One popular item in "head shops" is a harmless looking Coca-Cola can which has a false bottom. There is a frisbee available which will hide grass and has a "built-in" pipe for smoking pot.

• Look for books and magazines like "High Times" which are definitely pro-drug.

• Look for red eyes. Sometimes children come to school stoned or get high while in school. Favorite spots for smoking a joint are in a remote area of the schoolground or in the restroom. Youngsters may use eyedrops to remove the redness. One junior high student told us: "At parties we stop smoking grass about ten o'clock and then everybody starts putting Visine in their eyes." Look for "glassy eyes," dilated pupils, a fuzzy look. The child may have the appearance of looking "in the distance."

• Look for a sweet smell in the rest rooms or on children's clothing. You may smell the scent of burnt rope. At times you may smell alcohol on the breath.

• Look for compliant behavior. When people are high, they are usually more agreeable and compliant. Police often report that at rock concerts they encounter few fights. Marijuana tends to make the individual quite docile. Teachers should be alerted to youngsters who sit quietly (and seem removed from the situation) and smile weakly when spoken to.

• Fatigue and slurry speech. A funny or false laugh.

• Little sense of time. A child who is stoned has a distorted feeling of time. Events seem to be "speeded up." Ask a child to indicate the passage of one minute of time. A child who is high will usually think that a minute has passed after an interval of only 15 to 20 seconds.

In addition to the signs mentioned above, you may see the following — particularly after continued use of drugs.

• Number of friends decreases. Changes in friends. New friends that the youngster has not associated with before.

• Consistent drop in school performance. Less interest in school. No longer participates in class discussions. Does not complete homework. Less interest in school activities.

- A change in the standards of grooming. Less care about appearance.

- A change in behavior. More moody, less productive. If working, a major change in job performance.

- Less concern with home and family. Less and less time spent at home.

- More secretive. The youngster may give the appearance of hiding objects and seems very secretive. One sometimes sees feelings of paranoia in persons who are using drugs.

- A chronic cough or chest pains. Constant sniffing of the nose. These symptoms are usually not present in beginning pot smokers or beginning cocaine users. However, they may appear after continued use.

Finally, it should be emphasized that many of these symptoms can indicate problems other than use of drugs. A child who continually stays up late to watch television will show signs of fatigue and have redness in his eyes. There are many reasons why a child could get moody or begin to lose interest in school. The onset of the teen years can often create changes in behavior. However, in most children the onset of adolescence will be accompanied with heightened interest in several areas: more interest in the opposite sex, more attention to grooming and general appearance, increased interest in school functions and a new zest for life.

It is incumbent upon the teacher to be alert to all the signs mentioned above and to begin to ascertain the reasons which may be causing changes in behavior. Our experience has been that often children may be engaging in drug use ... but home and school either neglect or refuse to observe the obvious signs that drug usage is taking place.

What Teachers Can Do To Curb Drug Abuse

In spite of the major problems associated with drug abuse, teachers and parents *can* stem the tide and reverse the process. This section contains specific suggestions which have been useful in helping children cope with the drug problem. In addition the special bibliography at the end of this chapter contains references which describe specific programs where parents and the schools have cooperated and been successful in attacking the drug problem. The concerned reader is encouraged to study the references and to contact the organizations listed in the bibliography.

How to discuss drug & alcohol abuse with students

Hold discussions with children about drugs, drug use, and peer pressure. In too many instances, adults are prone to "preach" to children about drugs. Adults should have discussions and allow children to voice their concerns. In our research for this chapter, we have learned that most youngsters will openly talk about drugs and their role in teen culture. The teacher can provide some guidance by suggesting specific areas for discussion. For example: "The role of the peer group in drugs" or "Just say no...and the problems of saying 'No' when offered a drink or a joint" or "The effects of drugs on pregnancy," or "Alternatives to drugs."

Psychologists often use the term, "Concerned Listening" or "Active Listening." These terms mean that the teacher not only hears what the child is saying, but what the child is feeling. It means that the person listens to the comment, rather than thinking about their own response. It means that the listener — listens — rather than giving a quick or easy response.

Coupled with the concept of "Concerned Listening" is "Empathic Responding." This means that *after listening* — the teacher gives the person a response which shows that she understands how the individual feels and what the individual is saying. *All too often teachers are not good listeners. As the child is talking they begin to frame their own reply, rather than listening to the comment — and the spirit of the comment.* When teachers do not listen and do not show a real concern or empathy, they merely turn children away from them. They are, in effect, showing children that they really do not care.

In addition to the concepts of "Active Listening" and "Empathic Responding" there are two other techniques which can be helpful in communicating with others.

We have found one technique that is quite helpful in holding discussions and is particularly useful in teaching students how to hold a discussion. This method of discussion is called "Circular Response." The participants make a circle. The first person in the circle begins by talking about the subject. They may make any comment they wish. In some instances, there may be a time limit on each discussant's contribution. After the first person talks, the individual seated to that person's right has his turn. The discussion proceeds around the circle and each person must contribute.

The circular response technique does have two rules: First, the contributor cannot verbally disagree with any of the preceding statements. Second, if the individual does not have any new ideas, he must summarize the comments of the last contributor. The idea behind these rules is simple. If the person knows in advance that he cannot disagree, become negative, or get into an argument — he will listen since he must either *add* to the discussion or *summarize* the previous contributor's comments. Notice that this discussion technique is similar to empathic responding. It forces the participants to listen to the contributor rather that "cutting him off" or taking an adversarial position.

Another technique for effectively communicating with others is the concept of the "You Statement" and the "I Message." The "You Statement" has the effect of placing blame and creating guilt. The "I Message" has the effect of presenting a person with your own honest feelings and suggesting possible alternatives to the problem.

Examples: In the "You Statement" the teacher might say: "You are talking. Do you always have to run your mouth?" With the "I Message" the teacher could state: "I cannot teach class when you are talking; it is very difficult for the other children to hear."

Instead of: "You are a slow poke! Must you always be the last one to finish?"

Try: "I notice that you are having difficulty in getting finished. I wonder if we could find some ways to help you get your work done more quickly?"

Notice that the "You Statement" has the effect of criticism or incrimination. It sounds like an assault on the other person. In addition, the "You Statement" creates a negative emotional climate. It immediately places the child on the defensive and often makes them *reply* with a "You Statement" of their own! The "I Message," on the other hand, is given in a calm but firm manner. It shows the individual the problem with clarity and may provide the person some suggestions on ways behavior can be improved or altered.

Another helpful communication technique is the concept of "I win, you win." All too often we place people in an "I win, you lose" situation. This action usually places the individual on the defensive and he responds, "No you don't win, in fact ... I am going to win and you are going to lose!" Unfortunately in many "I win, you lose" situations, both parties may lose. The teacher should try to create situations in which both parties can win — and keep their respect.

Other suggestions

The best time to stop drug abuse is to approach the problem before it actually becomes one. The old adage, an ounce of prevention is worth a pound of cure, is especially

118

true in terms of drug abuse. We firmly believe that there will continue to be more outside pressures exerted on children to experiment with drugs at younger ages. Here are some additional suggestions which may be helpful:

1) Teachers and the administration need to compare notes in order to determine the extent of the problem in the school. Teachers need to identify areas both in and out of school — where drugs are being used and sold. In a number of situations we have found that the administration tries to pretend that there is no drug problem — somehow hoping that, if unnoticed, the problem will go away. We suggest that you consult resource people in the community who may be more familiar with the drug problem and can make concrete suggestions for dealing with drug abuse. Talk with social workers, psychologists, drug counselors in hospitals, medical personnel from specialized hospitals which deal principally with drug and alcohol abuse, persons in family and children's services, police officials and persons from the court system.

2) Teachers need to learn more about drugs and their consequences. The purpose of this chapter is to make the teacher cognizant of the seriousness of the drug problem and how to deal with it. As teachers we need to be aware of the dire consequences of drug use. It is difficult to give counsel to students when they know more about drugs than we do. Students often have only "partial knowledge." For example, most students will insist that pot is "less dangerous than cigarettes." Such statements actually avoid the issue. Cigarettes and pot are both extremely dangerous substances. Unless the teacher is well-informed, she cannot respond meaningfully to the student.

3) Help children learn more about drugs and their consequences. Children need to be more knowledgeable about

drugs and drug abuse. Three references which are particularly helpful to use with children are: Janeczek, C., *Marijuana: Time for a closer look;* Mann, P., *Marijuana update,* and Mann, P., *Twelve is too old.*

Youngsters should be made aware of the consequences of taking drugs. There is a large body of research available which conclusively shows that severe physical and psychological damage can result. Recent studies on marijuana, for example, show that continued use can cause memory loss, brain and liver damage as well as cellular metabolism and reproduction. Crack is highly addictive both physically and psychologically. The "high" associated with crack may last about five minutes. The feeling of euphoria is often followed by acute depression and an intense desire for another "hit." Cocaine can cause death by disrupting the brain's control over the heart and respiration. In a number of instances death has occurred with first time users.

4) We must recognize that children need accurate information about the problems of growing up in today's world ... who is really behind the drug traffic ... why? What about crime ... and its relation to drugs. Drugs are big business and organized crime does not care about the tragic situations which are created when persons become involved in drugs. We are not suggesting that you "scare kids to death," but to be more realistic about the problems in the world today.

5) Give children an accurate picture about their own physical and psychological development. Help children to understand the biological, social, and psychological changes which are occurring as they approach adolescence. While these changes often make growing up difficult, they lay the foundation for healthy adult development. Psychologists recognize that drug use   prevents teenagers from realistically addressing the problems of maturing.

Children need to recognize that the pre-adolescent and adolescent years represent a time when the child learns how to deal with adversity and change. Problems with parents, school, and the opposite sex are all normal parts of growing up. One of the major developmental tasks of the teen years is to learn to cope with stress and learn problem solving strategies. However, drugs interfere with this decision making process. Drugs cloud the issue— they cause the child to delay decisions and avoid reality. When he is high, his problems seem to disappear and the youngster begins to feel that drugs have "solved" his problems. Unfortunately this type of attitude inhibits an extremely important phase of growth and development and robs youngsters from experiencing the normal growth problems which are essential to future growth.

6) The importance of openness and acceptance. Children must realize that your approach to them is open and above-board. They must feel that they can trust you and that you are accepting of their ideas. For many children their teacher is the "Court of last resort." They realize that their parents and others will not accept them or their behavior – and the teacher may represent the only member of the adult world to whom they can turn for reassurance, counsel and advice.

7) Enlist the aid of parents. Many parents recognize the seriousness of the drug problem. Most of these parents are ready and willing to work in cooperation with the school to meet the drug problem "head on." Many parents are already concerned but do not know where to turn for guidance. When a parent finds their child is on drugs, there is usually a tendency to withdraw from other parents. Often there is a feeling of guilt and a belief that the problem is entirely their own fault. Parents may also have feelings of shame and experience difficulty in discussing the problem.

One of the most effective solutions to the drug epidemic has been parent groups. In most cases where parents have organized, compared notes, and attacked the problem in force, drug use has decreased. If your school does not have a drug problem, we suggest that you establish a parent network and conduct drug information seminars. Parents need to be informed about drugs and to alerted to the facts concerning drug abuse. The reader is referred to the special bibliography at the end of this chapter which lists specific references concerning the organization of parent groups.

8) Make students and parents aware of the school's drug policy. Students should understand that the school will not condone drug use, possession, and sale on school grounds and at school functions. Policies should clearly state what constitutes a drug offense and the consequences of a violation. The rules should specify what happens for a first offense and for repeat offenders. It is important for rules to be clear, firm and enforced. We also suggest that the administration consult with the school's attorney to ensure that policies are in compliance with local, state, and federal statutes. (Note: See the U.S. Department of Education's pamphlet, *Schools without Drugs*, for a discussion of legal considerations including search and seizure.)

More and more schools have recognized the dangers of drugs and are taking a "get tough" stance with clear, firm rules and swift action. In all cases where a "no nonsense" attitude has been enforced, drug use has been severely curtailed. Administrators may wish to query schools that have designed effective drug policies. Examples of schools with specific policies directed toward use, possession, and sale include: Anne Arundel School District, Annapolis, MD 21404; Northside High School, Atlanta, GA 30314; Eastside High School, Patterson, NJ 07509; and Greenaway Middle School, Phoenix, AZ 85001. There are other suggestions in the special bibliography at the end of the chapter.

9) Getting outside help. If there are already a lot of drugs in your school you do, indeed, have a big problem. As stated earlier in this section — the best time to stop drug abuse is to approach the problem *before* it becomes one.

Making a referral

However, if the problem already exists, the teacher needs supplemental aid and assistance. Unfortunately there are times when a teacher recognizes that one of her pupils is seriously "hooked" on drugs and that the parents are unaware that such a condition exists. Since the teacher is not adequately trained to handle this type situation, she needs to enlist the help of the administration, the parents, and other outside agencies. We have found that when a child is deeply involved in drugs, and may be a multi-drug user or into hard drugs, referral is an absolute necessity. Many schools have policies and procedures for handling this matter — and such procedures should be implemented immediately. We should point out that some parents may resent your suggestion that they need outside help. As mentioned earlier, the parent may feel guilty or even deny that a problem exists.

If your school does not have a policy for dealing with substance abuse, we would suggest the following: Discuss the problem with the principal and your school psychologist. If your district has a drug counselor, that person should be consulted. Since the teacher is often the only person known to the parent or principal caregiver, the teacher may need to initially talk with the parent and arrange for additional consultations with other school personnel, e.g., the principal, school psychologist, or drug counselor. In this situation it is probably best for the psychologist or drug counselor to make any referrals which may be necessary. Referrals can include having the parent make arrangements with the family physician for treatment, the appropriate social service agency, or investigating the possibility of utilizing a drug treatment center.

Since the problem of drugs is relatively new, most persons are not knowledgeable about treatment centers as a source of referral. Be advised that there are a variety of philosophical orientations related to methods of treatment and in some states referral centers and qualifications of staff may not be regulated. We would make the following suggestions in terms of evaluating a treatment program for young persons. 1) Check with your local medical and/or psychological association for referral suggestions. Query the family physician and/or your county health service about a specific facility. 2) Check the credentials and experience of the staff — usually there are staff members who are former addicts who understand the full extent of the problem. 3) Make sure that the staff is prepared to treat youngsters and has experience in working with youth. 4) Get a thorough evaluation of the extent and seriousness of the drug problem. 5) Program treatment should view chemical dependence as a primary problem. 6) Is there post treatment and follow up? 7) Since it is often advisable for the entire family to be in counseling, are there support services for the family?

If your school does not have professional support personnel, we suggest contacting city or county family and children's services or other appropriate agencies for assistance in ways to handle this problem. If your school system does not have a standard operating procedure, we would strongly suggest that the school board or central administration set up procedures for dealing with children who are addicted to drugs.

Alcohol and drug abuse represent the biggest problem ever faced by American education. Drugs are everywhere and impact on the lives of all our children and their families. If we do not move quickly and firmly we may lose an entire generation of youngsters to drugs. While the battle against these harmful substances is a difficult one, this chapter describes positive ways to combat the problem. We do know that in communities where schools and parents have combined their efforts, drug use can be severely curtailed and ultimated stopped.

Special Resource Bibliography on Drugs

Books & Pamphlets:
The books and pamphlets below will give the teacher a good beginning library. Materials which are (*) are particularly valuable.

*Barbour, J. (1981). *Marijuana and your child.* New York: The Associated Press.

*Bennett, W. (1986). *Schools without drugs.* Washington: U.S. Department of Education. (Note: Teachers may obtain a free copy of this pamphlet by writing to Schools without drugs, Pueblo, CO.)

*DuPont, R. (1984). *Getting tough on gateway drugs.* Washington: American Psychiatric Press.

Hawley, R. (1984). *A school answers back: Responding to student drug use.* Rockville, MD: American Council for Drug Education.

Janeczek, C. (1980). *Marijuana: Time for a closer look.* Columbus, OH: Healthstar Publications.

*Manatt, M. (1983). *Parents, peers, and pot II.* Rockville, MD: NIDA.

*Mann, P. (1980). *Twelve is too old.* New York: Doubleday.

*Mann, P. (1985). *Marijuana alert.* New York: McGraw-Hill.

Miller, J., Cisin, I., & Abelson, H. (1983). *National survey on drug abuse.* Rockville, MD: NIDA.

New Hampshire State Dept. of Education. (1979). *K-12 guidelines for school preventive drug education.* Concord: State of New Hampshire.

NIDA. (1981). *Adolescent peer pressure.* Rockville, MD: NIDA.

Rubel, R. A (1984). *A comprehensive approach to drug prevention.* Austin: National Alliance for Safe Schools.

Tobias, J. (1986). *Kids and drugs.* Annandale, VA: Panda Press

*U.S. Department of Justice. (1984). *Team up for prevention.* Washington: Drug Enforcement Administration.

Weekly Reader Publications. (1983). *A study of children's attitudes and perceptions about drugs and alcohol.* Middletown, CT: Xerox Educational Publications.

Organizations to contact for further information.

American Council on Drug Education (ACDE). Organizes conferences, develops media campaigns, reviews scientific findings, publishes materials. 5820 Hubbard Drive, Rockville, MD 20852.

Families in Action. Maintains a drug information center with extensive library. Publishes a newsletter. North Druid Hills Rd., Suite 300, Decatur, GA 30033.

National Federation of Parents for Drug-Free Youth (NFP). Helps organize parent groups; publishes newsletter. 8730 Georgia Avenue, Suite 200, Silver Springs, MD 20910.

National Parent Teachers Association (PTA). Has a variety of pamphlets related to drugs; planning guide for high school PTA leaders. 700 N. Rush St., Chicago, IL 60611.

Parents Resource Institute for Drug Education (PRIDE). Offers consultant services to parent groups, schools, and youth groups. Conducts annual conference. Woodruff Bldg., Suite 1002, 100 Edgewood Avenue, Atlanta, GA 30303.

National Institute on Alcoholism and Alcohol Abuse (NIAAA). Box 2345, Rockville, MD 20852.

National Institute on Drug Abuse (NIDA), Room 10-A-43, 5600 Fishers Lane, Rockville, MD 20852.

Learning Objectives for Chapter Five:

After reading Chapter Five, "Drugs: A special problem," the reader should be able to:

1. Have an overview of the drug problem in the United States.
2. Have knowledge of the incidence of drugs, especially as they impact on young children.
3. Name the four major drug categories: Depressants, stimulants, psychedelics, and psychotropics.   In addition the student should be able to list some of the common drugs and symptoms of excessive use.
4. Discuss the role of the peer group in terms of drug use.
5. In addition to peer group pressure, list other reasons which may lead to involvement in drugs.
6. Recognize "signs" or symptoms which may indicate drug use by youngsters.
7. Name the two basic models associated with drug addiction: the physical model and the psychological model.
8. Discuss several things teachers can do to help curb drug abuse. (The text lists nine things the teacher might consider. The reader should be able to discuss each suggestion and show how these could be implemented.)
9. Recognize the importance of discussing drugs and drug abuse. The student should be able to define the following terms and show how these concepts relate to group and/or individual discussions: Concerned Listening; Active Listening; empathic responding; circular response; "you statements" and "I messages."

Chapter Six

Classroom Management And The Exceptional Child

Virginia A. Boyle, Ph.D.

Within the school setting, exceptional children are classified as those children who have some physical, intellectual or emotional handicap which interferes with, or depresses learning and adaptation to school. The handicaps are seldom directly responsible for deviations in adaptive behavior in the sense that they cause the student to be aggressive, obstinate, uncooperative, withdrawn or overly active. However, attentional deficits, high or low activity levels, or emotional reactions and actions associated with the handicapping condition can directly affect the behavior of the student and the type of response he displays in the classroom.

It is important to recognize that exceptional children with any single or multiple type of handicapping condition are more like "normal" students than they are different. They are the same because learning is important to them, making friends is important to them, relating to the teacher is important to them, playing and having fun is important to them, feeling

128

worthwhile is important to them, and feeling that they have a contribution to make and something to give — is important to them. They have essentially the same feelings as other students in that they have happy, glad, sad, mad, frustrated, scared and anxious feelings. They react to situations most of the time with the same feelings — if they have difficulty learning, they become frustrated and feel bad about themselves; if they have successes they feel good about themselves. Just as with any student, they are hurt when someone is critical of their behavior or rejects them.

They are different from other students in several ways. For example, they may require: (1) some adaptation in the physical setting to accommodate their physical handicap, (2) some adaptation in material and informational presentation, (3) a specialized structure to help in prompting more appropriate, and efficient, behavioral responses to various settings. In addition, the teacher must be aware of the limitations associated with a specific handicap. In this manner the teacher can be more realistic about the quality and quantity of response she can expect.

Major Causes of Handicaps

It is important to understand that handicaps may be caused by a variety of agents or events. These can be categorized into basically four divisions: physical or biological, cultural, family rearing and educational.

Physical or biological causes have a wide range including: (1) some type of genetically related or congenital aberration such as Down's Syndrome or microcephaly which causes mental retardation, (2) a traumatic event which is directly insulting to the neurological system as in encephalitis associated with red measles, (3) a fall on the head which may lead to specific learning disabilities, mental retardation, deafness or blindness.

While the cultural milieu is not usually considered the precursor to a handicapping condition, it certainly can be one.

When a student comes from a different culture he may have to contend with language differences as well as varying expectations with regard to behavior.

Family rearing practices constitute a significant force in terms of the child's attitudes and behaviors. The family "sets the stage" by teaching the child coping styles which are used in dealing with an array of emotions and emotionally arousing situations. There is little doubt that the influence of the family has a major impact on the development of the child.

Education can be a causative agent of student handicaps. Research shows that the early years of education can predispose a student to like or dislike school, to feel motivated or not motivated to perform well in school, to feel trust that those important adults in the classroom will guide him in learning important basic skills. Moreover, should a teacher be poorly prepared to teach certain skills, the student may accumulate gaps in his educational experience. These gaps will handicap him in the mastery of other skills and knowledge. The mobility of the population can play a role in producing educational gaps because the student who moves about frequently may miss opportunities to learn certain skills.

Understanding the causes of handicaps and the associated behavioral management difficulties is beneficial in that methods of treatment sometimes can be aimed directly at the cause. For example, if neurological difficulties are responsible for an overly high activity level, and the student has a short attention span, a physician may prescribe medication which can increase the student's ability to attend to relevant information. Family practices and attitudes can be altered to bring about changes in the student's behavior. However, there are times that the casual agent is unclear, or unknown, or there is no known manner in which the cause can be affected. In these instances the teacher must deal directly with the behavior and utilize methods that modify or change the behavior.

In the process of deciding how student behavior is to be managed or changed, teachers tend to focus on the student as the object of change. *In fact, the first person who must change in the process of changing behavior is the teacher.* The teacher must change in her attitudes, expectations, goals, and responses to the student. In this process the *last* person to change is the student and only in response to those changes made by the teacher.

In guiding the behavior of the exceptional student, most management techniques — such as those listed by the authors — are equally effective with exceptional students. At times, however, some aspect of the student's handicapping condition may prevent the teacher from utilizing certain techniques or render these "usual" techniques less effective. When this occurs it is essential that the teacher reassess her approaches, expectations and setting.

Because exceptional children are typically more like "normal" than they are different, most "normal" management principles apply, but often must be emphasized more strongly than with normal children. Consequently, key principles will be listed below which, in many instances, are a repetition of ideas presented in other chapters of this book. However, they bear repetition and reiteration because of their importance in the management of exceptional children.

Key Principles In Working With Exceptional Children

1. Rapport or "Honey catches more flies than vinegar"

The necessity of establishing rapport with exceptional students bears much emphasis. It is an idea that teachers tend to forget particularly in times of frustration and stress. Exceptional students are people and, like most people, they tend to more cooperative with persons with whom they have established a positive relationship. Students wish to please those people whom they feel believe in them, have confidence in them and like them. Disapproval, correction and criticism from people they like, and by whom they feel liked, is more potent and more important to the student to avoid. Rapport is the power, the drive behind techniques of management; techniques alone are much less effective and some are not effective at all.

2. Modeling or "Monkey-see, Monkey-do"

In chapter three the authors have emphasized the importance of modeling as a major mode of learning. Students tend to mimic and imitate those behaviors they see other people use, particularly if those behaviors are effective in obtaining those things that the observing student finds desirable. Students are also inclined to imitate teacher behaviors and may adopt some behaviors as their own. This idea is particularly important when we consider that students learn how to cope with many feelings and problems through observing or even reading how others cope. Values, attitudes, morals, ethics and emotional controls are learned from others.

3. Consistency or "Just one more time"

Many teachers tend to believe that once a specific behavior has been punished or reinforced — that behavior should be eliminated or "permanentized" forever. However, this is not the case. In order to establish or alter a behavior pattern, one must consistently "water and fertilize" the grouping of desired behaviors. The newer the acceptable behavior or the older the unacceptable behavior, the more consistent the behavior modifier must be. For example, suppose the teacher wants a child to hold up his hand before speaking in a class discussion. It will be necessary for the teacher to prompt, redirect and reward that behavior daily until it becomes apparent that the behavior is well established. For some students, the behavior might become well established in two weeks, while other students may need on-going usage of these techniques over several years. This is particularly true of impulsive, hyperactive students who have to expend a great deal of time and effort in controlling impulses.

4. *Punishment and redirection or "Stop-Go"*

In behavior management, teachers tend to focus on undesirable conduct. While it is important for the teacher to identify behaviors which are inappropriate and which interfere with learning, it is even more important for them to identify acceptable conduct. When the student stops acting in one way, he will replace the extinguished behavior with another. The wise teacher is one who identifies appropriate behavior outcomes. If the teacher does not do so, the student is apt to elect to act in ways which are equally inappropriate and ineffective. Once a behavior is stopped through various forms of punishment, the teacher should provide structure, prompt or redirect the student to appropriate behavior and follow that behavior with a pleasant consequence. Research shows that this combination of techniques is one of the more effective forms of behavioral change.

External Factors that Provide Sources of Control

There are many factors within a school and classroom setting that can be used as a source of external control for students. Some of the familiar sources of control consist of rules of behavior and enforcement of these rules, the classroom curriculum (when a child is learning academic material, it is difficult for him to "act out"), curricular schedule, classroom routines, the physical arrangement of a classroom, directions from the teachers concerning classroom assignments and selective placement of students who have control problems.

Teachers seldom think of many of these as sources of control, yet they know that if they have not planned their "learning day" in terms of student needs and interests, they can expect more behavior difficulties that day. Thus, a teacher who invests time in developing daily lesson plans will be amply rewarded, particularly by those students who have control problems. These plans should include considerations of: what students need to learn that day, the skills the students need in learning the material, the length of time the student can likely attend to that material, the type of learning format which will claim attention and facilitate learning, the amount of material the student can handle in terms of self-direction and self-control and the interests of the student.

While these factors are true of "normal" students, they are even more relevant for the exceptional student. Exceptional children may have severe limitations in the knowledge and skills they bring to the learning situation. The special child may need extra cues in the learning presentation, selected types of learning formats, as well as more frequent breaks in learning due to a short attention span and greater fatigue. Exceptional students may not be able to respond to some types of formats because they do not have the self-motivation or self-control to utilize them. In addition this student may need greater amounts of warmth and encouragement from the teacher in order to persevere when they feel so discouraged about their abilities.

Classroom control is, in the mind of many educators and lay persons, associated with the degree of punishment which a teacher or administrator has at her fingertips. While many different forms of punishment are certainly needed in the classroom, they should not be considered the major source of classroom control. For the exceptional student, who may have greater difficulty in establishing emotional and behavioral controls, this would mean more negativism—and an increased loss of self-respect. It could also result in negative attitudes toward learning, the school and the teacher. Control is most effectively established when it offers the student direction plus information on ways he can accomplish what is expected. Positive control speaks to those techniques used by the teacher which not only direct and instruct the student in what is expected, but those which offer support and encouragement to do so. This can be provided through the learning situations teachers establish, the types of structure utilized, plus the recognition and praise given the student when he is performing as expected. Students need rewards and confirmations for those things they do which are right more than they need punishments for things which they do which are not desirable.

There are many other types of external controls which can be utilized by the classroom teacher. Some specific suggestions are outlined below:

1. Follow difficult, frustrating assignments with activities which are rewarding and which offer the student a means of energy and tension release. For example, providing each student with a sheath of old newspapers which they can tear vigorously on command for one minute (and clean up the mess afterwards); foot or potato sack races outside; the vigorous and lively singing of songs. To effectively use these activities, it must be made clear that the "acting out" student may have to be relieved of the opportunity to participate in the activity or the entire class may lose the opportunity. This includes waiting patiently for an activity to start on teacher command and stopping promptly when terminated. It also includes responsibility for clean up.

2. Using students to recognize and praise other pupils when they are acting as expected and ignoring them when they are violating an expectation or rule.

3. Role playing can be used in activities where the expectations are explained to the students and role played. This is a particularly helpful activity to employ when expectations are complex and where students need to be prompted to respond to teacher cues such as hand signals.

4. The teacher should be alerted to transitions. Remember that transitions offer the greatest opportunity for misbehavior. This is particularly true for the exceptional child. Transitions should be well-planned and expectations made clear. For example, if a class does not handle the transition to lunch as quietly and smoothly as needed, the teacher may need to review the entire procedure with her students. She may wish

to introduce some type of structure which aids in a transition. The green table can go; the red table is quiet, so it can go." The teacher may wish to have the children "role play" the transition and give recognition when students respond appropriately. In the next chapter, the subject of transitions is treated in greater detail.

5. Use "positive thinking" exercises with your students. Have the children sit quietly for a few minutes, heads on arms, in a relaxed position — "just like a loose, limp Raggedy Ann doll." While in this mode, ask them to *really concentrate* on how they are going to do a certain task — how they are going to feel in doing the task, the effort they will expend, how satisfied they will feel when they have accomplished their goal. This technique is particularly effective with a new assignment or when a task may be difficult and frustrating.

From External Control to Internal Control "Yours to Mine"

When students are misbehaving in the classroom, and interfering with learning and classroom procedures, it becomes necessary for the teacher to establish outside controls or structures which aid in reducing or eliminating inappropriate behaviors. Classroom rules are an example of such an external structure. In training students to improve their behavior it becomes important to develop a system whereby the rules and reinforcements begin to belong to the student, that is, they begin to become "internalized structures." In the final analysis, this is the "bottom line" —we want our students to be able to abide by the rules because they see the need to do so. In Chapter Seven, the concept of internal and external discipline will be explored in greater detail.

1. Student punishment may be punishing to the teacher

In selecting behaviors which must be stopped by punishment, it is important for the teacher to choose punishments that are easy to apply. If the action becomes painful for the teacher, she will be less apt to employ the techniques and become inconsistent in treating the behavior. For example, the teacher may say, "Buddy, it you do that one more time I will have to send you to the principal or I will have to severely punish you." If the teacher does not really want to send the student to the principal because it could make her look badly in his eyes or if she does not want to severely punish the student because it is painful for her to act in this manner — she will be most reluctant to follow up on her threat. Buddy then learns that he can continue to misbehave with little fear of the consequences.

It is also important to realize that in most instances the punishment does not have to match the deed in terms of power or intensity. It is important, however, that the deed be punished — and punished consistently — if it is to be extinguished. Thus the key is selection of a punishment which is consistent with the teacher's philosophy and one which she can apply consistently with little or no hesitation. In the final analysis, it is not necessary for the teacher to be punished when the student is punished.

2. Be a good scout: Be prepared

Teachers seldom do a lot of behavior management planning prior to the arrival of new students. Usually they do not think through the acceptable or undesirable behaviors they may witness — nor the reinforcements which might be appropriately meted out. This type of preplanning is beneficial, however, since it will expedite student adaptation to the classroom. In teaching exceptional children it is particularly important because of the higher incidence of maladaptive behavior that is associated with this group. (See Figure 6.1)

Prior to opening day, the teacher should make a list of potential nonadaptive behaviors which she may expect from her students. It is also helpful to list comfortable punishments and redirections which she feels would be effective in teaching students the desired behaviors. Teachers tend to become emotional and overreact when they are presented with student behaviors which they did not expect and feel incapable of handling. As the teacher becomes more skilled in dealing with nonadaptative behaviors, she will be better equipped to handle them without becoming overly upset.

Figure 6.1
NEGATIVE BEHAVIORS ASSOCIATED WITH
EXCEPTIONAL CHILDREN

Exceptionality	*Key Characteristics*
Learning Disabled (L.D.)	Hyper or hypo activity, negative attitudes, testing behavior
Mental Retardation (M.R.) (Mild)	Passivity, non-initiating, testing of limits, limited social skills
Emotionally Disturbed	Wide variety of symptoms. May display, every characteristic of L.D. Extremely fearful, crying, selective mutism, explosive episodes, acting out, tantrums
Visually Impaired	Overly dependent, extremely shy, fearful, withdrawn, explosive episodes, self-stimulating behavior, tactile behavior, mobilization problems
Hearing Impaired	Loud, acting out, socially limited, communication difficulties, withdrawn
Neurologically Impaired	Language delay, loud abrasive, limit testing, erratic behavior, high activity level, explosive episodes, impulsivity, short attention span
Chronically Ill Asthmatics, diabetics, etc.	Quick fatigue, low energy level, psychosomatic complaints, overly dependent

3. The more regressed, the more structured

There are occasions when a teacher becomes heir to an immature class of students — or a situation where many members of the class are "late maturers." When this occasion arises, the teacher must recognize that these students have fewer internal controls and thus need greater external control and structure. The teacher needs to increase those structures and directions with firmer direction and redirection. The teacher may have to resort to employing a more rigid and traditional classroom arrangement. She will need a greater array of comfortable punishments and redirection. In addition, she will have to work constantly to discover the positives in those immature students in order to provide them with the positive reinforcement, rapport and encouragement which they need.

4. Power Struggles: The winner may be the loser

At some point every teacher has some students who present themselves as belligerent, defiant and test the teacher's authority. There are some hyperactive children who give this appearance but who, in fact, are simply not aware of the boundaries or the rules. That is, they are not intentionally setting out to defy or overrun the authority.

There are other students, many times children with learning difficulties or emotional problems, who have established a pattern of defiance and limit testing. They may argue with the teacher over various issues, they may deliberately participate in an act of defiance or they may persist in trying to obtain special privileges.

These kinds of students are particularly difficult for teachers to handle because of the emotions they arouse in the teacher — usually as a result of their subtle or blatant disrespect for the teacher's authority. It is difficult for the teacher not to react by getting sucked into a power struggle with the student. The teacher may begin to argue back or begin to make strong assertions of her authority by being punitive. It is true that once into a power struggle, the teacher must win, but in winning she has also become a loser in that she will begin to lose her objectivity and effectiveness with the

139

student. In losing the battle, the student feels put down and may become angry toward the teacher.

Therefore, it is important for the teacher to recognize those times when the gauntlet has been thrown out by the student. Perhaps the most helpful clue to the teacher in identifying the potential onset of a power struggle is by being aware of her reaction to the student. When the teacher feels threatened and frustrated by the student there is always a possibility that a struggle is "on the verge."

How does one respond to a ploy by the student which would initiate a power struggle? The teacher can simply ignore the comments and acts of the student. She could verbalize what she thinks the student is doing — comment on what she thinks the outcome might be, and then indicate her desire not to become involved in a situation which would lead to those kind of results, and then ask the student what he really wants. Sometimes merely asking the student to verbalize the rule or the expectation will bring a halt to a power struggle. The issue then becomes — different approaches the teacher can develop to avoid the power struggle.

Supplementary Factors That Contribute To Student Control

1. Medication

Medication can prove useful in reducing the high activity level of a hyperactive student or the anxiety of an emotionally disturbed child. The use of medication in management of behavior has been over emphasized by educators and there has been a resulting backlash on the part of parents and physicians. It is not the professional responsibility of the teacher to determine whether a student would benefit from medication; that responsibility belongs to the physician and parent. All the teacher can be responsible for in relation to medication is suggesting to a parent that they consider consulting their physician for examination and recommendation. A teacher is not professionally licensed to administer the medication, even though many do and are placing themselves in jeopardy by doing so. They can keep medication for students and make it available to them.

There are some hyperactive children who, on taking the proper type and dosage of medication, change dramatically in their behavior. There are others who can attend somewhat better and we may see some improvement in behavior. There are some children whose behavior has not improved and they may even be more active as a result of medication.

2. Cooperation of the home

Parents of exceptional children often feel guilty and responsible for their child's handicap. They can easily become defensive about problems which arise in school and become uncooperative with the school. At times they may attempt to blame the school for their child's difficulty or may attempt to avoid any discussions about the problems their child is presenting in the classroom. In their attempt to undo or deny their child's handicap, they may be overly protective and quite unrealistic about their expectations for their child and his teacher.

One of the biggest complaints parents of exceptional children have is that the only time they are contacted by the teacher or school is when their child is presenting problems. For some students who are having major adjustment difficulties, these calls may be quite frequent. If the teacher can stand back and look at what is being said, she may realize that in developing any type of working relationship, it is better to start off on a positive note rather than a negative one.

If a teacher knows of a student who may present problems in the classroom, she should contact the parents and take the time and opportunity to visit with them before the child's problems are discussed at a future conference. Via notes and telephone contacts, the teacher should take the time to

141

provide the parents with positive feedback on the areas in which their child is doing well. (Refer to the bibliography. The chapter on troubled children by Gearheart and Weishahn has some excellent suggestions on parent communication.)

Throughout the school year the teacher should work to provide the parents with a balanced, but realistic picture of their child's progress. The teacher should be very open about the problems she sees with the child in his role as a student. The focus should be objective and should not cast blame on the parents or the teacher. It is perfectly acceptable, even desirable, for the teacher to identify problems the child presents with which the teacher is having difficulty. Often parents can make constructive suggestions to the teacher by sharing techniques which have worked well for them. The relationship between the teacher and the parents should be one in which both identify problems that need attention and on which they can work together to arrive at solutions.

3. Psychotherapy and counseling

There are times when a student can benefit from psychotherapy or counseling with a trained mental health professional. The parents and entire family may also need some professional help. A suggestion from the teacher can often prompt the parents to investigate whether this type of service is needed.

Once a child, parents or family are in psychotherapy or counseling, there may be important information which the teacher and mental health professional can share. Information can be shared between parties only when the parents give their consent. Needless to say, all information shared is highly confidential as is all information that a teacher normally has available on a child. This information should not be discussed with anyone who is not professionally involved with the child without the consent of the parents.

4. Special education services

Many exceptional students are eligible for various types of special educational services. Services can range from psycho-educational evaluation to consultation with the classroom teacher to placement, either partial or full-time in a special education class or program. Special education services are always a supplementary program to the regular classroom unless the student utilizes special education services more than half the day. This means the regular classroom teacher retains responsibility for the instruction the child receives. At times there may be disagreement between the regular teacher and special education personnel as to how a situation should be handled. Of course, it is best to work out some type of solution or compromise to avoid placing the student in a situation where he suffers from the conflict between professionals. If this is not possible, it is wise to bring in administrative personnel — and if necessary the parents — to aid in resolving the conflict. The conflict should never be allowed to interfere with instruction and management techniques being provided to the student.

5. Tutors

There are times when a student can benefit from tutorial instruction outside of school. The parents may be unable to help their child with homework assignments or projects without undue pressure or frustration. Tutors can sometime aid in helping the child establish work-study skills which are unknown to the parents. As such, it is to a teacher's benefit to develop a list of tutors who are reputable, conscientious and work well with youngsters.

In summary

It is hoped that these suggestions, techniques and key principles will be helpful to the teacher as she works with the exceptional child. However, as we mentioned in the beginning of the chapter, *it is important to recognize that exceptional*

factors or areas in the classroom milieu which can affect student behavior.

Figure 6.2
FACTORS WHICH AFFECT CLASSROOM BEHAVIOR

1. Degree of rapport teacher has established with students, or is in the process of establishing.
2. Physical arrangement of the classroom.
3. Instructional placement of student:
    a. Should be at or below instructional level. Remember that most tests give us frustration levels which are higher than instructional levels.
    b. Look for skill gaps.
    c. Motivation of student to learn.
4. Relevance of curriculum.
5. Type of structure introduced by materials and activities; it determines the behavior a student must use to complete an assignment.
6. Use of selected assignments to shape up desired behavior.
7. Frequency of transitions and transitions needing structure.
8. Identification of assignments and activities that lend themselves to disruptive behavior.
9. Verbal structures provided by teacher.
    a. Description of what a student is expected to do (directions).
    b. Clarity of description (directions).
    c. Prompts
    d. Redirection
    e. Rules
    f. Enforcement of rules (including threats).
10. Overplanning of assignments (not busy work).
11. Established routine.
12. Alternation of activities between highly desirable and those low in desirability.
13. Length of assignments made; must take into consideration short attention spans.

14. Pacing of activities; i.e., teachers rate of movement through activities.
15. Use of contingencies: "Good things happen when you are good; bad things happen when you are bad."
16. Use of grades and scores in motivating students.
17. Use of active learning.
18. Presence of intrinsic reinforcements in material and activities and use of extrinsic reinforcements when intrinsic ones are low.
19. Percentage of positive statements made by teacher to students. (# of positive statements, gestures, movements/ Total # made. — 60% ratio recommended).
20. Use of peer control.
21. Use of groupings.
22. Use of variety in instruction.
23. Anticipation of endings.

In summary

It is hoped that these suggestions, techniques and key principles will be helpful to the teacher as she works with the exceptional child. However, as we mentioned in the beginning of the chapter, *it is important to recognize that exceptional children with any single or multiple type of handicapping condition are more like "normal" students than they are different.*

Learning Objectives For Chapter Six:

After reading Chapter Six, "Classroom Management and the Exceptional Child," the reader should be able to:

1.   Recognize that the exceptional child is more like the "normal" child than different.
2.   Identify and list the four major causes of handicaps: Physical or biological, cultural, family rearing and educational.

3. Without the aid of references, list and discuss _____ key principles which are important in working with exceptional children. Note: The text describes ten key principles; readers can set their own criterion for adequate knowledge of this item. These key principles include: the importance of rapport, modeling, consistency, punishment and redirection, internal and external factors, structure and struggles for power.

4. Discuss some of the negative behaviors that may be associated with exceptional children.

5. Discuss the teacher's role in terms of medication.

6. Discuss the importance of working closely with the home and family.

Chapter Seven

Techniques of
Classroom Management

Perhaps the single most important factor in controlling classroom behavior is the teacher's ability in making the subject matter stimulating and enjoyable. When this is accomplished, children become involved and teachers experience few discipline or management problems. When teachers present their subject matter material in interesting and relevant ways, children will be attentive. If, on the other hand, the learning climate is dull; the discussions irrelevant; the material too advanced; the assignments inappropriate — students become bored and frustrated. The result? Children start to misbehave.

Our research has shown that sometimes teachers become so busy and ego-involved, they are totally unaware of their own behavior. At times, the teacher may unknowingly use rough techniques; she may avoid the aggressive child; ignore the passive individual and devote a disproportionate amount of time to the cute, verbal, attractive youngster. Teaching is a very difficult job — teachers have to juggle many factors and constantly change and adjust their priorities. In Appendix D, we have included some items which are designed to help the teacher assess herself by analyzing her teaching methods and determining if she is meeting her overall goals.

Warmth, friendliness and enthusiasm are important to effective classroom management and discipline. When teachers treat children like "somebody" with warmth and friendliness, children will do the same in kind. We can establish good lines of communication by treating children with mutual respect. Teachers need a repertoire of verbal and non verbal ways of communicating with learners. Appendix A has several suggestions for verbal and non verbal reinforcers.

The earlier chapters of this treatise have been primarily directed at discipline in terms of the individual child. However, the principles and techniques which have been discussed are, for the most part, equally applicable to small groups or to an entire class. For example, consistency is important whether or not the teacher is disciplining a single individual or a total group. As mentioned in Chapter Four, rough control techniques are generally detrimental and actually have no greater effect in gaining compliance than do milder influence techniques. The principles of reinforcement theory are also appropriate in class settings and can aid the teacher in the utilization of group management techniques. In addition, there are some strategies which one should consider when working with an entire group. The purpose of this chapter is to examine these areas and their implications for the teacher.

Contagion Effects

In Chapter Four we discussed the ripple effect in discipline. We noted that the ripple effect is the influence a control technique exerts — not on the target child — but on the other children in the classroom as the IT "ripples out" from the target child. Chapter Four discussed several effects in this connection: When the IT was clear — and the IT was firm, the audience children responded with increased conformance. On the other hand, when the teacher employed techniques which were harsh or rough (e.g., being angry, highly punitive, shouting), the entire class become apprehensive, less involved in their work and showed general signs of anxiety and restlessness. The ripple effect studies were conducted with elementary school children. However, one of the authors conducted a similar study with high school students and obtained the same results. That is, when the teacher used rough, harsh techniques the class became apprehensive and the level of work was impeded.

In other words, there is a contagion factor in classroom management. Therefore, the teacher must be aware that children can also learn the rules of behavior indirectly — as they observe the manner in which the teacher disciplines others in the classroom. The following examples may be helpful.

Ms. Bales is working with a reading table. At an adjacent table three boys are playing with a lotto game. One boy, apparently bored with the game, pushes his lotto cards on the floor and leaves the table. Ms. Bales looks up and says, "Clark, come back and pick up your mess." At this instant, Ms. Bales is distracted. Seeing that the teacher is not looking, Clark turns around and goes to the easel. Roscoe, a second boy at the lotto table says, "Ms. Bales, Clark didn't pick up his cards." Ms. Bales does not respond.

Roscoe shrugs his shoulders and scatters his cards on the floor. Marvin, the third boy at the table, laughs and begins tossing cards in the air saying, "It's raining lotto ... it's raining lotto!" Annemarie happens to be walking by the table. She picks up several cards from the floor, tosses them in the air and mimics Marvin, "It's raining lotto ... it's raining lotto!" Roscoe picks up the lotto box and hits Annemarie over the head saying, "Get outta here ... this is our game." At this moment, Ms. Bales looks up from the reading table and says, "What is going on here?"

Ms. Days, a student teacher, is giving directions for a science experiment to the entire class. During the lesson Gail and Coy periodically whisper to each other. At one point Grace joins in the conversation. Evidently Coy says something funny because Gail and Grace begin to snicker. Grace turns to Wilma, at the next table, and whispers something to her. Wilma looks at Coy and starts to laugh. Coy and Gail start to laugh aloud. Grace whispers something else to Wilma and both start laughing. Ms. Days stops her lesson and says, "Grace, I saw that!"

In the two examples presented both teachers were negligent in pursuing any definite course of action. As a result, deviant behavior began to spread. In the case of Ms. Bales, she failed to "follow up" on her original admonition to Clark. Upon seeing this, Roscoe duplicated Clark's behavior. Marvin likewise became contaged and drew Annemarie into the misbehavior which finally resulted in her being accosted by Roscoe.

Ms. Days, the student teacher, waited too long and permitted the misbehavior to spread. Starting with Gail and Coy, it soon encompassed Grace. Shortly thereafter the misbehavior spread to Wilma at a nearby table. Wilma, in turn began to laugh and her laughter rippled back to infect the original twosome.

Let us examine one more episode: Ronnie had problems prior to his arrival at school. He and his mother had a disagreement and he arrived at school angry and upset. When Ms. Purvis greets Ronnie he just scowls and bulls his way into the room. He approaches the block area and pushes Byron to the floor. Byron complains verbally and kicks down a block tower. Ronnie then shoves Lesley into Grady. Grady pushes Lesley to the floor and punches Ronnie. At this moment, Eula is passing by with a doll in the baby buggy. Lesley tips over the buggy.

In the meantime Ronnie and Grady are having a first class fight. Grady hits Ronnie in the mouth and Ronnie screams, "You blooded me!" He feels his lip and confirms that there is a trace of blood. Crying loudly, Ronnie retreats toward Ms. Purvis for comfort. Meanwhile, the classroom is in shambles.

Unfortunately Ms. Purvis failed to notice that Ronnie was angry and upset. Had she recognized these early warning signs, she could have directed Ronnie to an activity away from other children until he felt better. Instead, Ronnie's anger ultimately had an impact on the entire group.

Establishing Discipline and Classroom Management

It is our opinion that the first two weeks of a school program are crucial in terms of effective discipline and classroom management. The teacher must plan the classroom in every detail and establish expectations related to behavior. As the teacher looks at the room from the child's point of view, she must think through details concerning placement of equipment, where coats will hang, how the furniture will be arranged. She must also determine avenues of movement and easy accessibility to her pupils. By analyzing the structure of the classroom, she can forestall many logistical problems. The teacher should prepare name tags for each child. She needs to label individual materials and must have a record keeping system in place which allows for effective management. She must think through the schedule from the point of entry into the classroom, to the point of exit. Each academic transition should be planned, including a good balance of quiet and active periods. Planning also includes decisions concerning where children will be allowed to eat snacks, library procedures, bathroom procedures, lunch room duties, and auxiliary personnel must be considered. A daily schedule should be posted as well as fire drill and evacuation procedures.

The first day needs particular attention. It sets the stage for the rest of the year. The room should be ready for the children and should be inviting, colorful, and suggest a climate which motivates children to learn. Some teachers find it effective to write a welcoming letter to their students. In the letter the teacher should tell a little about herself and what to expect on the first day. The teacher may wish to suggest that the child bring a sharing item for the first day.

Preschool programs are much more effective in terms of planning for entry procedures and do not require that a grand scale reorganization take place each Fall. Many schools have initiated a staggered enrollment which allows for an easier transition. It is much more desirable to stagger entrances which will allow teachers a lower pupil-teacher ratio during the first few days of class. When the teacher faces 20-25 new faces each year, the first few days must be structured differently in order to establish a safe and trusting environment.

In most instances we like for rules to evolve from the classroom and from the children. We believe that children like to be involved in the democratic process of rule making. However, during the first few days of class, it is generally necessary for the youngsters to know what behavior is expected of them. The teacher needs to have a list of behaviors which she expects from every child and she should inform children of her expectations. In the preschool and early primary grades, it is necessary to spend more instructional time on teaching rules and expectations. These expectations should be clear, positive and concise. After the first few days — as the class experiences problems, students should be involved in making rules which will help the class to run efficiently.

We do not agree with the old adage, "Don't smile until Christmas." However, it is necessary in the beginning to make a conscious effort to enforce the rules, and remain firm. If the teacher lacks organization or lets children initiate control, the year can be a disaster for the teacher and the entire classroom. The teacher should exhibit an attitude of being warm and friendly which communicates that she is in charge of the learning process and she cares about each individual and his or her needs. It is much more difficult to regain control from a classroom which has already learned how to control the teacher.

Routine duties which the teacher must accomplish such as lunch reports or attendance should be analyzed to determine the most efficient way to achieve the tasks. When children can read their names, they can accomplish some of the tasks without teacher assistance. We saw a neat clothes pin chart which allowed children to take their pin and place it on the chart for attendance. One teacher went one step further and divided her chart into columns. One column was for students who wanted a regular lunch and the other was for children who wanted the salad bar. The child placed his clothes pin with his name on the chart according to his selection. This chart was done with pictures to assist children in placing their clothes pin in the appropriate column. It was easy for the teacher to count the number of children who wanted regular lunch or salad and required little interaction or time for her to fill the report which went to the lunchroom.

We have been delighted to see lunch room personnel take responsibility for collecting money and keeping records related to the lunch room. The decision to assign a lay person this task should enable more teaching to take place and help maximize the time on task for students. If you have the responsibility of keeping lunch records, design a format which allows children to assume some of the responsibility and ask parents for help to insure the process takes the least amount of time necessary.

A posted schedule, with pictures for nonreaders, is helpful. The first few days make reference to the schedule and discuss procedures. Learning routines and the order of the day help the class to run smoothly. Children need the security of knowing what to expect and when they will transfer from one class to another.

It also helps to think through all the different jobs which children can do in terms of routine tasks and establish a system which allows children to know when it will be their turn to be door holder, line leader, fish feeder, helper, etc. During the first few weeks of school it is necessary for the teacher to fully explain each duty in order for the child to know what is expected and the teacher must follow up to be certain that each duty is fulfilled. The more the teacher is able to allow the children to maintain the classroom, the more teaching time will be available for the class.

Transitions and Movement Management

Teacher attributes include liking children, being creative and possessing knowledge in several subject matter areas. In addition the teacher needs to be an efficient manager. Jackson (1968) found, in an average day, the teacher may make 200-300 individual child contacts and supervise a dozen activity changes. Kounin (1970) observed that elementary classroom teachers averaged 33.2 major changes in learning activities in a single day! Thus, the teacher must be able to help children make many new shifts each day. These transitional changes not only require new equipment and materials but also entail a psychological alteration in one's frame of reference. These shifts can involve physically moving desks and tables; getting out new books; putting away play materials, plus cognitive shifts to problem solving, inductive reasoning and a host of other mental exercises. Teachers need to be aware of the impact that transitions can have on the tempo of the day and the potential for class disruption. In addition, teachers must remain alert to individual and group needs. The school day should be well balanced to offer variety, reduce boredom, and maintain interest.

Kounin (1970) and Gump (1982) investigated movement management in greater detail and the reader is referred to their research for a thorough analysis of this area. Kounin's categories related to movement include: smooth transitions, jerkiness, flip-flops, and stimulus-bound events. In this section we will review these categories plus some additional areas which the authors feel are germane to good classroom management.

1. Transitions

There are three stages to most transitions: 1) "the close" — closing the current activity, 2) the "changeover" — the move to a new place or a new activity and 3) "the open" — beginning a new activity. As indicated earlier, a teacher makes many transitions during the course of a day. There is research to suggest that when the three stages are structured and well-defined, transitions occur more smoothly and efficiently. When transitions are not performed efficiently, they can consume a great deal of time and cut into educational activities. Gump (1982) reports that noneducational functions can range from 21 percent to 40 percent of the school day. Good & Grouws (1975) found that effective teacher managers made fewer transitions and spent less time in effecting a transition. Often the manner in which transitions occur (smooth, jerky or abrupt) can effect the tone of the class. For example:

The class is outside on the playground. Ms. Sauls says, "All right children, it is time to go inside! Doris you will be the leader and start the line indoors." In this example, Ms. Sauls' influence technique is quite clear. It also possesses a certain definiteness and her directions are quite specific. The children will probably go inside without too much trouble.

Let us now examine a second observation: The class is outside on the playground. Ms. Schuler surveys the playground and says, "All right children, in five minutes we will go inside." Seeing that Diane and Robert are deeply involved with the outdoor blocks she adds, "Diane, you and Robert will have to stop in a couple of minutes so you will have time to pick up your blocks." Like Ms. Sauls, Ms. Schuler's influence technique was quite clear. It was definite and specific. However, Ms. Schuler's overall transition (from outdoors to indoors) appears to be smooth. She surveyed the group and provided a warning. On the other hand, Ms. Saul's approach to the transition appears abrupt and jerky. But, we might ask, does this minor difference in approach to a transition really make any difference. Kounin's work and the research by Good & Grouws would suggest that it can make a difference in children's behavior. Ms. Sauls appears to be "butting in" on the children's activities. Research suggests that jerky, abrupt transitions are more disturbing to children and create a situation more likely to contribute to deviant behavior. Certainly experienced teachers would advise: Whenever possible, give children a "warning" in preparation for a change or transition in activities.

A transition effects the behavior of both pupil and teacher. Arlin (1979) found that the rate of pupil off-task behavior was nearly double during the "changeover" stage of the transition. Likewise, Gump (1969) found that teachers made more behavior corrections during a transition.

We have a few suggestions to help effect smoother transitions. It usually helps to warn children of an impending "close." This gives youngsters an opportunity to finish their present activity. Make the close definite so students know that a close is taking place. Recognize that during the second stage, the "crossover," there is usually less structure and more movement activity. This is particularly true if children are moving from one classroom to another; from outdoors to inside; from the gym or lunchroom to another class. In these situations, deviant activity is more likely to occur. Krantz and Risley (1977) found that when children went from recess to a quiet activity there was a large increase (37%) in off-task behavior. However, when the authors inserted a short resting time prior to the new activity, the off-task behavior was greatly reduced. In starting a new activity, an effective "opening" helps prepare your students. Help pupils get quiet and do not begin if there is a lot of extraneous activity. Determine if your students have the appropriate materials — the correct book, a pencil, scissors, glue.

The "opening" should get the attention of the students and include the purpose of the lesson. Many times we have observed teachers jumping into the heart of the lesson without telling students why it is important to learn the material. If the student is not motivated or does not understand the need to acquire this specific knowledge, the lesson will not be successful. Once the stage for learning has been established, the teacher should ask one child to repeat the purpose for the lesson. This technique requires all students to listen and the teacher can evaluate how effectively she is communicating.

Hunter (1980, 1981) points out that when teachers reduce the empty waiting times during transitions they are more effective She recommends a technique called "sponge activities" when waiting for class to begin, dismissal of class, waiting for materials to be passed out, waiting to go to other locations such as lunch, library, assemblies. A sponge activity absorbs the dead or idle time in the classroom by changing the wasting time to learning time. It may provide practice for needed concepts, establish the stage for the next lesson, or lessen discipline problems and potential disruptions. A sponge activity requires minimal materials and directions, starts and ends at any point, all abilities may participate, has content validity and is fun. Examples of beginning sponge activities include listing animals that live on ___, clapping games, or scrambling spelling words then swapping with a friend to solve. A dismissal sponge could include flash cards with correct answers earning dismissal, being able to give four basic shapes, say a word which begins or ends with a specific sound, dismissal by eye or hair color, apparel, or birthday.

We also suggest that the teacher analyze transitions by observing behavior of the class. If the teacher is well planned and not thinking about the next lesson or getting materials prepared, she can more effectively execute transitions. Particularly at the beginning of the year it is helpful to time transitions. Some teachers have found it helpful to set a timer toward the end of the lesson. She may state that they have five minutes to complete an assignment. She sets the timer and

157

the ding indicates that they should be ready for the next activity. She also may ask for a show of hands to determine how much time to allow for the completion of an assignment.

2. Stimulus-boundedness

Kounin contrasted stimulus-boundedness with goal directed behavior. In a goal directed situation the teacher maintains her focus on a specific goal; in a stimulus-bound event the teacher reacts to some unplanned or irrelevant stimulus and is lured away from the original event. For example: The teacher is at the chalkboard explaining a math problem. She looks down one aisle and sees a piece of paper on the floor. She says, "Who dropped that paper on the floor? This room is becoming a pig pen." She walks over to the paper, looks at one of the children and says, "Mario, did you throw this paper on the floor?" Mario shakes his head and the teacher leans over and picks up the paper. She dramatically shows the paper to the class and says, "Here is a mystery for you. How could this piece of paper walk from someone's desk and find its way to the floor?"

Another example of "stimulus-bound" behavior can be seen in the following: Ms. Duggan is listening to Eva read aloud. As Eva is reading, Ms. Duggan is walking back and forth in front of the room. She looks up from her reading and notices the animal cage and exclaims, "Eunice, you forgot to feed Harvey." Eva stops reading as Ms. Duggan goes to her desk and gets some rabbit pellets. She offers the pellets to Harvey saying, "I bet you are really hungry!"

Certainly there are situations which demand stopping a teaching activity. Often, however, teachers become stimulus-bound and distracted to some new situation which is totally irrelevant. In both examples presented there is class disruption — work activity stopped and children were impeded from continuing their academic pursuits. In both cases, however, the class disrupter — the work stopper — was not a deviant child. Rather, it was a stimulus-bound teacher.

3. Flip-Flops

Kounin uses the term, "flip-flop" to describe the following situation. The teacher terminates one activity, starts another and then abruptly returns to the original activity. For example, the teacher says, "Put away your arithmetic workbooks and get out your science books and turn to page 87." After the children have their science books open the teacher says, "How many of you finished your arithmetic problem?"

Another example of a flip-flop follows: The Hawks have finished their reading. The teacher says, "Okay, you may take your chairs and return to your tables." The children rise and start to return to their tables as directed. The teacher then says, "No, wait ... come on back and let's finish the story we started on Tuesday."

A flip-flop is actually a transition that it is jerky and abrupt. Like the stimulus-bound event, it is disruptive and prevents the class from progressing smoothly. In a flip-flop the teacher has terminated one activity — started another, and then reverted to the initial activity. We might also refer to flip-flops as "changing horses amid stream." This type of transition is very disruptive to the class and our own research has shown that all teachers engage in flip-flops. Kounin's research indicates that avoiding flip-flops will enhance work involvement and lessen deviancy.

4. Herding

Some teaching experiences are reminiscent of the old Texas cattle drives. It involves moving children — from one table to another, from the homeroom to the bathroom; to the music room; to the auditorium; as well as daily trips to lunch and the playground. Teachers can devise methods which will ease movement problems and make transitions smooth. At times movement can be tied to concepts in problem solving. For example: "All who are wearing blue can go to the bathroom; all who are wearing green ... Monday's row may go; Tuesday's row ... "

On field trips peer arrangement may be a more crucial consideration. The teacher may wish to designate one child as leader (or head) of the line. The teacher will usually wish to hold the hands of specific children who may become frightened, have a tendency to forget rules, are impulsive — or children who have a tendency to run and create a "child stampede!"

Significance of Movement Management

We cannot over-emphasize the importance of movement management. Studies show that effective teachers are also good managers in terms of the various transitions which occur during the school day. Since so much of the school day is involved in movement management, it becomes a significant dimension in control and guidance in the classroom setting. Teachers who make abrupt transitions, flip-flop and become stimulus-bound will experience discipline problems and general disruption. Poor management techniques consume time which can be used in more productive ways. The teacher should carefully analyze her approach to change and transition. The importance of this area is emphasized by Kounin (1970, p. 108): "Techniques of movement management are more significant in controlling deviancy than are the techniques of deviancy management as such."

Pacing, Spacing and General Management Considerations

The teacher has been compared to an orchestra leader, the president of a business, an agent of culture, a maintenance man, a janitor, and a traffic cop. In many ways there are elements of all these tasks embodied in the teacher's role. The teacher has many functions to perform. In addition to guiding many activities throughout the day the teacher must "pace" the day to avoid satiation and boredom. She must be alert to the many activities which are taking place simultaneously; she must be aware of both group and individual needs.

160

Effective teachers are able to "look ahead" and move to prevent problems before they occur. They recognize the importance of voice modulation as a management technique and the need to get the active attention of the entire class when providing instruction and information. All of these activities and materials must be considered in perspective or the teacher will find herself involved in "fighting windmills" and in "over-kill." This section will consider many of the general management considerations to which the teacher must remain ever alert.

1. Fighting Windmills

There are a number of conditions which occur in life (and in the classroom) which could mercifully be termed "circumstance." Fighting windmills refers to situations in which the teacher may become upset over a condition which she is unable to control. Examples of this situation are: Getting upset when the floor gets muddy on a rainy day. Trying to maintain absolute silence in the lunchroom because the principal enacted a law stating, "No talking in the lunchroom." Taking children on a field trip and saying, "I want it so quiet I can hear a pin drop on this bus." Expecting children to be calm the day before a holiday.

There are many windmills in the teaching profession. If the teacher allows herself to become overly concerned, she can actually do damage to herself psychologically and physically. In the school setting, windmills usually occur in two areas: One — in the case of an administrative ruling over which the teacher has no control. Several years ago, we did a study on stress (Osborn, 1984). We found that one of the biggest factors in teacher stress was related to administrative decisions over which the teacher had no authority or control. The second "windmill" exists in situations where one expects more of children than they can reasonably deliver. Our advice: Relax, "roll with the punches," try to maintain a sense of humor; keep important issues in perspective and retain some feeling of equilibrium.

Thus, children do get muddy shoes and they will become excited the day of a Valentine party. Talking at lunch is not deviant behavior; it is human behavior — and kids are like that — they are human.

2. Buildups and slow downs

The teacher must be alerted to the overall pace of the day. A day should be well balanced so that vigorous activities are followed by a quiet period of time. Activities involving quick rapid strenuous physical movement should include periods where the child can relax and rest. A school day is not paced like the TV show, "Wheel of Fortune." Children should not be expected to operate on a "high" the entire day. In many instances a deviancy problem may be related to pacing. According to Gartrell (1987), effective teachers avoid prolonged adult-directed lessons that place children in passive roles.

Let us observe the pacing (or level of activity) during a typical morning. Usually the activity level of a class starts slowly. As the morning progresses, however, the activity level (and the noise level) begins to build. One of the advantages of snack time or recess is the opportunity it affords for a change of pace. It gives children a chance to slow down, relax and engage in quiet socialization. During the course of a busy morning the teacher may not have had occasion to speak to each child. Snack time provides the teacher with a well-timed opportunity to interact with every individual.

Following snack period the activity level begins to build again. As lunch time approaches the activity level usually moves to a higher pitch. In addition, as children become hungry, frustration tolerance is lowered and tempers can flare. Just prior to lunch the teacher should plan some event (stories, songs, books, puzzles) which calm children before going to eat.

Discipline and pacing are highly correlated. Problem situations arise when a group of children have been involved in vigorous activity over a period of time and find it difficult to slow down and "return to normal." Teachers should also carefully schedule activities so that children will not have extremely long waiting periods. Long waiting periods can be very frustrating to children and create unnecessary disturbances. Equally difficult are situations where children have remained quiet over a long period of time and have been unable to move about the classroom. As mentioned earlier, Hunter offers several excellent suggestions to aid the teacher in utilizing the wait time with "sponge activities."

A teacher should have some "pace changing" activities in her repertoire. The purpose of the "pace changer" is to quickly alter the activity level of the class ... thereby preventing a discipline or management problem. The teacher should learn several of these activities so well that she can institute them in a moment's notice. There are two general types of "pace changers" — one is designed to increase the activity level of the class; the other is designed to help the class lessen its pace.

Pace Changer Number One: Letting off steam. The purpose of this activity is to encourage children to move around, jump up and down and generally lessen the tensions which can build in a classroom setting. Ways of reducing tension include a simple running game or a song game which utilizes gross body movement. There are times when a class has been engaged in an assignment involving concentration over a long period of time. In order to avoid satiation, the teacher may wish to change the pace for a few minutes and then return to the original activity. In this situation the teacher will wish to encourage movement, and yet maintain total control of the pace change. An example of this type of controlled activity is, "Simon Says." Notice the change of pacing in the following:

Simon says, "Wiggle your fingers."
Simon says, "Stretch your arms."

Simon says, "Run in place." (Then, if the children become
too boisterous ...)
Simon says, "Stop running."
Simon says, "Tiptoe quietly to your seats."

In this type of activity the teacher can allow movement and activity. Yet the class remains in control when it is time to return to the original task.

Pace Changer Number Two: Putting the lid on. Tension can also build when young children are involved in highly active games or competitive events. Over an extended period they may become highly excited and over-stimulated. When this situation occurs the entire class can quickly lose control and the group will seem to "fall apart." Even for the experienced teacher, returning to normalcy can be a difficult task.

Prior to the point where the class loses control, the teacher should begin initiating activities which lower the tension level. In some instances the teacher may wish to use a game (like Simon Says) which will begin to restore control and order to the group. Then as the group "slows down" the teacher might read a story, lead the class in songs or encourage activities of a more sedentary nature.

Another important consideration in terms of pacing and timing is the preparation and celebration of major holidays. If a teacher begins to celebrate Thanksgiving the first part of November, it will seem like an eternity before it arrives. This is particularly true for young children. It keeps the class operating at a "fever pitch" for an extremely long period of time. Since children do not possess the temporal relations of adults, this situation also creates problems in the home.

3. Geographical considerations

An important factor in behavior management concerns the placement of activities and materials within the classroom. General considerations for room arrangement include:

- Traffic patterns
- Noisy and quiet areas
- Space for large and small group activity
- Materials conveniently located
- Movable furniture
- Wet and dry areas
- Locker placement
- Window placement and glare
- Door placement
- Distraction factors from outside visible or auditory sources
- Storage facilities
- Color
- Balance and order
- Aesthetic appeal
- Ease of movement in relation to individual desk placement

In the fall of the year — before the opening of school, plan your overall traffic patterns and the areas which will be designated for different activities. The general considerations listed will help you as you do your specific planning. In terms of placement of specific items and activities the following hints may be helpful. The block corner should not be adjacent to the music corner. Even the normal "noise" which accompanies block building is too disturbing for someone who is endeavoring to listen to recorded materials. Note: A small carpet for blocks and transportation toys will reduce the noise significantly.

Easels should be placed in a well-lighted area; near a window, if possible. Easels and fingerpaint tables should be located near a water source and there should be a drying rack nearby for hanging completed pictures. Recently the writer visited a nursery school. The teacher of the four year olds had the easel paint drying rack across the room from the painting area. Hanging the pictures entailed walking the entire length of the room and through the dramatic corner. Not only was the rack inconvenient, the teacher disturbed the children in the dramatic area each time she went to hang a picture. Careful planning can save the teacher time and energy.

Be aware of the location of the sun throughout the school day. Will there be excessive glare on the desks; will the sun be in the children's eyes and interfere with their seeing the chalkboard or participating in other activities?

How much material will be in the room when it is fully equipped? At times teachers forget how much space tables, chairs, easels, doll beds, and blocks can consume. Then, when the room is completely furnished, there is no room for the children —or the room looks crowded, messy and unattractive.

The teacher should consider the placement of mats for rest period. Positioning of children is an equally important consideration. Children can become both physically and psychologically confined. When this situation arises, nerves become frayed —shoving, tussling, and fighting soon follow.

In primary classrooms teachers often place individual student desks in a pattern which makes it difficult to maintain eye contact with every student and, at times, impedes the ability of the teacher to walk quickly to the child who is causing a disturbance or having difficulty. Often proximity of the teacher to the child can make the difference in forestalling a problem. The writers have seen desk placements which allow the teacher ease of movement and still keep each student within easy reach of the teacher. We have also seen situations where the teacher had to walk "around the world" to offer support to students who were across the room. It is sometimes necessary to consider strategic desk placement of certain children who influence each other. The movement of a child's desk should be done without making an issue or allowing the child to lose face.

4. Over-kill

This technique refers to the teacher who makes a big issue out of some minor incident. The teacher engages in lecturing, preaching, or moralizing to the class. Generally this technique disrupts the class, slows down the class activity and may actually cause deviant behavior to occur. The writers recall a classic example from summer camp.

The "Eagles" (a ten year old group of boys) are playing the "Women-Haters" (an eleven year old boy's group) in a spirited game of softball. Royce, the counselor for the Eagles is coaching from the sideline. Wally, one of his campers, is playing third base.

Royce: "Okay, Wally, let's look alive."
Wally: (Looks at Royce and smiles faintly.)
Royce: "Come on, Wally, talk it up."
(Twenty seconds pass.)
Royce: "Hey, Wally, get ready — move around."
Wally: (shrugs shoulders)
Royce: "Hey, Wally, get ready —tough hitter, let's go!!"
The ball is hit to third base. Wally fields the ball and throws the batter out.
Royce: "All right, Wally, next time throw faster. He almost got on base."
Wally: (frowning) "Gosh, I got him out — what do you want? Give me a break!"
Royce: "Well, you could have missed him — look alive out there!" (Twenty seconds pass.)
Royce: "All right, Wally, get ready, talk it up, baby!"
Wally: (curls lip — says under his breath) "Get off my back."
Royce: "What's that? Get on the ball, Wally . . . Tough batter . . . Big stick!"
At this moment the batter rips a ground ball between Wally's legs. The runner advances safely to first base.
Royce: "Dammit, Wally . . . I told you to look alive. Get that apron down. . . you let them get a hit . . . get ready, baby, get ready!"

At this point Wally removes his fielder's glove, throws it in the air, and rolls on the ground. Royce looks at the observer, throws up his hands and says, "What the hell did he do that for?"

In the classroom setting we can see "over-kill" in the following example:

Feron is slow in coming to the reading group. Ms. Waldrop says, "Feron you are a slow poke. You are always the last one to the reading group. Everyone has to wait while you dawdle and take your own sweet time." Ms. Waldrop looks over the room and says to no one in particular, "What would happen if everyone arrived late?" Cecelia says, "We wouldn't finish our work." Ms. Waldrop, "That's right; Cecelia, we would never be finished. What would have happened if Paul Revere was late?" (no response) "What would happen if your house were on fire and the firemen arrived late?" (no response).

In this observation, the recorder commented that as the lecture on "being late" continued, the children were looking at the ceiling or the floor — and seemed to be purposefully avoiding the teacher's gaze. The observer also noted a slight undercurrent of noise. Often the preachments of "over-kill" disrupt the class and do not improve the behavior of the deviant child.

5. *Developmental differences*

Brophy and Evertson (1978) have identified three general stages of intellectual and social development which have implications for kindergarten and elementary classroom teachers. Stage one, kindergarten through grade 2 or 3, describes children as compliant and oriented toward conforming and pleasing their teachers; however, they need to be socialized into the student role. They require more formal instruction in terms of rules, expectations, room procedures, and routines. In stage two, grades 2 - 3 through grades 5-6, students have learned most of what they need to know about school rules and routines. Generally they continue to be oriented toward obeying and pleasing their teachers. Thus, less time needs to be spent in classroom management at the beginning of the year and less time is needed for cueing, reminding and instructions. Stage three, grades 5-6 through grades 9-10, describes children as they are entering adolescence and are less oriented toward pleasing teachers. In stage three, youngsters attempt to please the peer group and experience more peer group pressure. Many become resentful and question authority. Disruptions are frequently due to attention seeking, humorous remarks, silly comments, and playful teasing. Classroom management becomes more time consuming and motivation or controlling students is more difficult.

6. Self-help activities

If you closely examine your room and carefully plan your activities, you will discover many situations where children can perform tasks without teacher assistance. Train yourself to view each task as a production engineer. You will be amazed at the number of tasks children are able accomplish independently.

For example: Ms. Zeleny was the teacher of twenty-five four years olds. She had one assistant, Ms. Kay. Dressing to go outside was a major hassle. Ms. Kay would take the early dressers" (about three children) outside, leaving Ms. Zeleny with the rest of the group. The dressing room was very small. Fights broke out daily. There was always a mad scramble to get Ms. Zeleny to help. Finally Ms. Zeleny decided to approach her problem from a "production" point of view.

Each day Ms. Zeleny assigned several children to be "layout" assistants. Then, while she told the group a story, the layout personnel helped Ms. Kay place the clothing on the floor in the playroom. The clothing of each child was placed in a specific order. Snow pants first, then the boots, then the hat, followed by the coat and the mittens. The children enjoyed this activity and being chosen a layout assistant was considered an honor. Ms. Zeleny also alerted Ms. Kay to the importance of child placement. Children who were quite active were geographically separated to avoid fights. In addition, children who could dress themselves were placed next to children who could not — so the "dressers" could assist the "learners."

When the children started dressing to go outside, Ms. Zeleny and Ms. Kay were able to place themselves strategically. When a child was dressed, the teachers would show him another child he could help.

Dressing became an effective group management project instead of a teacher hassle. By making dressing an enjoyable experience in which children helped each other, there was a noticeable improvement in the *esprit de corps* of the total group.

Closely examine your room and your materials to determine ways children can help themselves. Here are a few examples to guide your thinking:

• *Clean up* — This suggestion is so basic that the teacher may feel it is unnecessary. Yet as we visit classrooms, we are surprised at the lack of "follow through" on the part of some teachers. Many teachers are continuously involved in picking up after children because they do not take the time to teach children their own responsibility for clean up after completing an activity. Granted, it does take time and patience to get children to learn this task. At times the teacher may need to offer encouragement and assist a child in this task. Children should learn, and the teacher should insist, that before moving to a new activity, they must pick up the material used in the previous activity. The teacher will save herself many precious minutes if she teaches children this basic rule in classroom management. It is also important for the teacher to be a good role model. If the teacher leaves her desk in disarray, students will follow her example.

• *Low labelled shelves* — Label positions for materials so children can replace items after they have been used. Utilize pictures for nursery school and kindergarten children. This technique teaches children classification skills as well as returning things to their proper place. It also builds a sense of security when children can depend on finding material in a logical, predictable order.

• *Bulletin boards* — Several children can be assigned the responsibility for decorating the bulletin board. The bulletin board should be positioned so children can easily reach the board.

• *Snack period* — Even two year old children can be taught to prepare for snack period with some assistance. These children learn sets and one-to-one correspondence as they learn that each child receives one glass, one napkin, one placemat, one cookie. They learn sequencing when they see that the placemat must precede the glass, etc.

• *Mixing paint and dough* — Teach children how to mix their own paint and assemble their own art materials. Containers should be accessible and have snap lids.

• *Library committee* — A library committee can be designated to choose books for the room and to keep them in an orderly state.

• *The new child* — It is often helpful to the teacher and security for a new child if he is assigned a "special friend" to help "learn the ropes" at a new school.

• *Parent help* — Parents can provide assistance in many ways. Parents can serve as "extra hands" on field trips, they can also assist in class on special days or school events. In addition, parents should be informed that there are many "little" ways in which the teacher can be helped. For example: Labelling clothing, purchasing galoshes amply large. Parents do not realize how frustrating it is when teacher and child have to struggle with a pair of tight overshoes. The same is true for other items of wearing apparel —coats sufficiently large for growing children; zippers that work; elastic pants; avoiding "Sunday" dress clothes, dressing the child in clothing that is washable. Self gripping fasteners are modern day wonders for teachers with children who have not learned how to tie their shoes.

• *Operating equipment*— Young children can learn to operate a computer, record player, tape player or a language master. Kindergarten children can operate headsets and be trained to operate most audio visual and office equipment. With the availability of rental agencies and video tapes, most young children have had opportunities to operate video equipment. Upper grade children are often more adept at handling AV equipment and following the rules which allow the equipment to remain operable. Teachers frequently are so busy keeping the class on task that they unplug the projector before the fan has cooled the bulb. The teacher who trains students to operate AV equipment will have more teaching time; and the administrator who permits tudents to operate the equipment will often discover fewer repair and replacement costs.

• *Assign tasks*— Our own experience is that teachers usually do not realize how well children like responsibility and how well they can accomplish complex assignments. There are many tasks which children can perform which will significantly reduce teacher load. In the children's camp at The Merrill-Palmer Institute several years ago, campers were primarily responsible for every phase of camp life including the planning, operation of the camp store, purchase of equipment and other camp functions. Younger children can dust, clean tables, distribute rest mats, and other materials. They can even call the roll and check attendance. As children grow older they can collect money, take up tickets, assume responsibility for the care and feeding of plants and animals, tutor younger children in subject matter areas and help supervise the day of these youngsters.

• *Cooperative planning* — A technique used successfully by many teachers is one of cooperative planning of activities and routines. This approach teaches children responsibility as well as providing an introduction to democratic planning and discussion. We suggest that you choose a routine or activity and lead a discussion with the children on the goals of the activity, the requirements involved, and the responsibility of the children involved. For example you might select activities like using the cafeteria, a fire drill, or the child's own use of free time. After the discussion, the major goal and the rules and responsibilities can be summarized and written on a large sheet of paper or poster board.

For example, if you are writing a plan for a fire drill, you might have as major goals, "To proceed safely from the building and assemble at a safe distance from the building. To insure that every member of the class is out of the building." After the goals have been established, you help the children determine both individual and group responsibilities necessary to achieve the goals and the procedures involved in arriving at the goals. These might include: being careful as you leave the room to avoid shoving or pushing; to walk on the right side of the hallway to the appropriate exit; to proceed to a certain area on the playground; to form a circle, and to call the roll. Insofar as possible, rules should be stated in a positive manner.

After the planning sheet has been completed, it should be displayed prominently in the room. Prior to a fire drill, the teacher and pupils can review the chart. Upon completion of the drill, the chart can again be studied to determine if the rules were followed and the goals attained.

This approach to cooperative planning helps the teacher to pinpoint a particular problem and to show the group, or a specific individual, where the procedure went awry. Thus it serves as a vehicle for correction of a problem situation plus affording children the opportunity to participate in democratic planning and discussion. Abiding by rules made under democratic procedures lays the foundation for future self-discipline and responsibility.

During reading group time, one first grade teacher was experiencing difficulty due to constant interruptions. She discussed the problem with the children and they developed a plan which eliminated most interruptions. This plan made certain that the teacher had the attention of the class when she was giving directions for independent work. She would ask another child to repeat the directions to verify they were understood. Then, if a youngster needed help, he would do the following: First, the child had to sit and think about the problem; then look to see if he could complete part of the assignment, or go on to another task. If, after completing all he could do, he could quietly ask a peer. If he still needed help he would go to the "big question mark" hanging from the ceiling and stand patiently until the teacher acknowledged his presence. When it was convenient for small group instruction to be interrupted, the teacher signaled she was ready to answer the child's question. This procedure eliminated many interruptions and created better work habits. The teacher felt that the plan increased the children's attention span and encouraged independent work habits. Another teacher had a question card which children used at their seats. Between small group work the teacher would monitor those with questions. Each teacher noted that writing directions on the board at the child's reading level was helpful.

Children at the primary level need to be encouraged to complete tasks independently and utilize problem solving skills. A chart can be a helpful reminder which encourages children to utilize problem solving strategies prior to seeking teacher assistance. Finally, it should be pointed out that when you encourage children to find alternate ways to solve problems, you must be prepared to accept their solutions. Children often develop creative strategies which may be quite different than the routine solution which the teacher expected. However, we believe that these creative endeavors which encourage autonomy and creative thinking are helpful to both teacher and student. Some of the serendipity in teaching is observing the original approach to problem solving that young children possess.

7. Are you "with it"?

Kounin used the term "withitness," to describe a teacher who could demonstrate to her pupils — "I do know what is going on!" The competent teacher can communicate (often via non-verbal means) — "I am aware of what is happening; I am in control of the situation."

Every teacher knows that disruptive behavior will usually stop when the teacher moves in close geographical proximity to the deviant child. However, beginning teachers tend to forget this premise and do not place themselves strategically — or they become involved in one situation — and forget about the rest of the class.

In successful management of the class, the teacher who is "with it" is capable of juggling the multi-faceted situational variables which prevail at any given moment in the school day.

External and Internal Discipline

Very early in life the infant learns that discipline is external to his own being. Even when he is very demanding, the control he exerts over his parents is entirely volitional — they can do as they wish; they establish the rules and they enforce them. It should be recognized, however, that in the case of the very young child the parent often has no other workable alternative. If a two year old is playing with a bottle of furniture polish, the parent will prohibit this activity. She will not consult the child and reach a democratic decision. This is as it should be ...no two year old is capable of understanding the dangers involved ...nor should he be consulted in the decision making process.

External discipline — while it may be very necessary — is not without problems. It is usually effective only to the extent that the authority figure, who imposed the rule, is capable of inflicting punishment.

For example, if the two year old is slapped every time he touches furniture polish, he will not touch the bottle under two conditions:

1) He sees the authority is present and knows that he will be slapped for his behavior.

2) He sees the authority is not present. However, the child fears that the authority may appear; and recognizes that, if the authority figure appears, condition (1) will prevail.

Given the previous example, the child's ability to discipline himself is based on circumstances which are external to him. In this instance, he will avoid the furniture polish because of fear of the authority figure.

In the final analysis, however, discipline must be considered in a larger context than merely in terms of reward and punishment. In order to be effective during those periods when the authority figure is absent, discipline must have meaning for the child.

When the child is older, the adult can explain the dangers inherent in a bottle of furniture polish. Once the child understands this fact he will refrain from playing with the polish because the reasons are meaningful to him. Under these circumstances — when discipline has become internalized — the authority figure does not need to be present.

Self-discipline begins to occur when the adult provides reasons for rules and regulations. Unfortunately, as cited in this book, adults often give prohibitions — but they seldom offer reasons.

In less potentially dangerous situations, children should be afforded the opportunity to learn rules through discovery as they explore and experiment on their own. Rules about living with others and working with others are often best learned in this fashion.

For example, Ms. Paguio was having difficulty with the concept of sharing in her first grade class. Usually the children resolved the problem of sharing via brute force. After a few weeks the teacher realized she has become the final arbitrator in most of the classroom disputes.

One day, during group time, Ms. Paguio raised this problem with the children. During the ensuing discussion the children compiled a list of "rules for sharing." One child suggested that these "rules" be posted on the bulletin board to serve as a reminder to everyone. After the children had agreed on the rules for sharing, disputes noticeably declined.

Children usually display pride and a feeling of *esprit de corps* when they share in making rules. The teacher should enlist the aid of the class in making rules which effect everyone.

Every time we help children learn to cope with a problem and to handle their feelings, we move them one step closer to mastering self-discipline. Self-discipline implies self-respect for others. We like Gartrell's (1987) approach to discipline problems with a solution orientation. When conflict situations occur a solution orientation means providing information so that children know what to do instead of what not to do. The goal is to help children solve problems. We once had a large four year old who virtually took anything he wanted from his peers. We talked to him as well as the group about using words to get children to share and be friends. We knew we were making progress when he charged toward a small three year old who had a truck he wanted. The timid three year old in his strongest voice said, "Use words, use words!" The four year old stopped in his tracks. As he paused for a instant it was obvious that he was engaged in deep thought. After a moment he offered to share his car with the three year old. Then, the two boys hugged each other, as if they had always settled confrontations with words. That's progress and a solution orientation!

Children can begin to learn social responsibility early. Although they are highly egocentric — and it is difficult to see another's point of view — very young children can begin to share and interact with others. If children are to learn social responsibility there must be many opportunities to test and to try; to succeed and to fail.

A major task for the parent and teacher is to structure the environment so that the child can begin to direct his own behavior within that environment and learn to live with the consequences of his own actions. Ideally, self-discipline is learned at home and in the classroom. In these situations the adult can create a climate which is basically trusting and friendly.

Discipline and Classroom Management Syndrome.

In this book we have examined many factors which are necessary for good discipline and management control. Current research and clinical observation would suggest that there is a "Discipline and Classroom Management" syndrome composed of behaviors which are used by teachers who are successful. To cite all these behaviors would involve reviewing the entire book. However, some factors seems so significant we would like to summarize the salient features of this syndrome:

• There is no substitute for good teaching. When subject matter is stimulating and enjoyable, the teacher will experience few discipline problems. Successful teachers present smooth, well paced lessons and make learning interesting and exciting.

• A major key to classroom management is prevention. Teachers who are effective disciplinarians and managers are able to prevent problems before they occur.

• Children do learn by modeling. Children model their behavior after the adult who teaches them.

• How you were reared as a child; the influence techniques used by your parents, your teachers; how you feel about discipline — all relate directly to your own attitudes and beliefs about discipline. Your attitudes have a direct relationship to the discipline techniques which will be successful for you.

• Recognize that human behavior is very complex. Often the causes for behavior may not be immediately apparent, but have their roots in physical, cultural or social factors which indirectly influence classroom behavior.

• The emotional climate in which discipline occurs is more significant than the technique used.

• The first few days of school are extremely important. Early planning is crucial. The early weeks create the initial climate for learning and set the stage for the remainder of the school year.

• Management techniques — particularly those involved with transitions and classroom change — are more significant in controlling deviancy than discipline techniques as such.

• In managing the classroom the teacher recognizes the value of organization and preplanning. The day should be planned well ahead of the children's arrival so the teacher has the time to greet the children and get them started toward a productive day. In preplanning the teacher considers:

— balance of activities
— variety of activities
— pacing

179

— individual and group needs
— short and long range goals

• In utilizing influence techniques, the teacher recognizes the importance of: clarity, consistency, and firmness. Effective teachers have clear rules and procedures and are explicit in the requirements of desirable behavior. The most effective teachers are consistent; they are less likely to ignore deviant behavior when it occurs.

• An influence technique will be improved if the teacher uses her "power" with a cushion — e. g., offering an alternative; an explanation; a reason.

• Children learn in accordance with the rules of reinforcement theory. Praising a child for appropriate behaviors, increases the likelihood that the desired behaviors will continue.

• Reward appropriate behavior after it occurs. Grandma's rule states, "First you do what I want you to do, then you may do what you wish to do." Usually the child will work for the opportunity to engage in an activity he enjoys.

• Reward the total class for appropriate behavior. Often the teacher takes good behavior for granted, but punishes incorrect behavior.

• Recognize the power of "positive statements." Catch a child doing good!

• Self-discipline occurs when children are provided reasons for rules and regulations which have meaning for the child. The ultimate goal is internal discipline.

In the final analysis, the teacher is trying to "work herself out of the business of discipline." In a democratic society authority figures do not follow people around enforcing rules, dispensing tokens and inflicting punishments. Thus, as the child grows into adulthood, he must develop an internal discipline. He ultimately learns to behave in an appropriate fashion—but not because of the teachers, policemen, parents and other reinforcers in society. He behaves appropriately because he lives in a society which respects fairness and honesty for oneself and for others.

Learning Objectives For Chapter Seven:

After reading Chapter Seven, "Techniques of classroom management," the reader should be able to:

1. Identify the single most important factor in controlling classroom behavior.
2. Identify contagion in a classroom and predict its effects.
3. Understand and grasp the significance of movement management and transitions in controlling classroom behavior.
4. Given a situation reflecting a problem in management or transition, the reader should be able to recognize an example of a stimulus-bound event, a "flip-flop," a problem of pacing and offer suggestions to improve the classroom management situation.
5. Discuss your strategy for preplanning and planning for the first few days of school.
6. Given a discipline problem related to the classroom environment, the reader should be able to analyze potential difficulties in room arrangement and make concrete suggestions for change.
7. Give examples of student "self-help" activities which can alleviate some potential discipline problems.
8. Discuss the concept of internal and external discipline. How can teachers help children learn to manage their own behavior?
9. Evaluate the authors' discipline and classroom management syndrome. Are there any additional points you would add to this statement?

Appendix A

Positive Verbal and Nonverbal Reinforcers

"One liners" that turn kids on ...

Every child needs praise and positive reinforcement. He needs to know the teacher cares for him as a person and recognizes his feelings and accomplishments. Unfortunately, adults often fail to reinforce desired behavior. At times we fall into the rut of using general vocabulary which does not meaningfully describe appropriate behavior or accomplishments. Teachers often say, "You are a good boy," when it would be more appropriate to describe the exact behavior or state specifically why the teacher is satisfied. For example, "You have really improved — you got all the problems correct!"

At times it is not what one says but how they say it. Positive reinforcements should be sincere, honest and enthusiastic. Some teachers utilize positive verbal reinforcers effectively, but may forget how effective the nonverbal gestures can be. Smiling, laughing, nodding, a pat on the back, or being close to a child can serve as powerful reinforcements. The teacher who learns to utilize verbal and nonverbal reinforcers will find them helpful in discipline and classroom management.

182

The following "one liners" and gestures are given as a beginning repertoire:

Teacher satisfaction — Verbal reinforcers
Thank you very much.
Terrific
You are very thoughtful.
Super
I appreciate your help.
Wow
That's wonderful.
Super duper
Good for you, _____.
Wise choice
Great—Hey, that's great!
Splendid
That's attractive.
Keen
You are tops.
Fine and dandy
That's a great idea.
Jam-up
I'm happy for you.
Thrilled
You are a gem, pearl, plum, etc.
Hmmm!
You win first place for that.
Hot digity!
I'm glad you did.
Splendid
That's pretty.
Fantastic
That's top notch.
Excellent
You're one in a million.
Neat
That's really helpful

Magnificent
I'm so pleased.
I'm tickled pink.
Swell
I'm so glad.
Nifty
I'm pleased as punch.
O-kay!
That's top drawer.
Goody
What a pleasant surprise.
Hot dog
I knew you could do it!
Oh boy!

Verbal reinforcers which acknowledge the child's accomplishments or ability

I can tell you are trying.
That's creative.
I can tell you are thinking.
I wish everybody could do_____!
You're a good problem solver — you can _____.
You worked hard on _____.
Your effort is evident.
I like the way you think.
I like the way you try.
I wish every room could see that — let's put it in the hall.
Let's show _____ to the principal or teacher down the
hall, or next level teacher, etc.
You did so well, you're ready to _____.
That's your best work!
You followed directions.
You do that so well.
You are really fast.
I can see you took your time to do that correctly.
You are doing much better.
You got it.
I like your drawing, it _____.
Hey, you got _____correct!

Keep up the good work.
That's better.
You're a good worker — you _____.
You are really improving.
You are smart to think of _____.
You have your thinking cap on.
You are to be commended.
Give yourself a pat on the back. Good job!

Verbal reinforcers which acknowledge child's feelings

I know you are happy inside.
You seem very happy doing that.
You seem pleased with yourself.
I can see you are really turned on.
You are happy as a lark, king, etc.
I can tell you are satisfied.
I know you are glad that _____.
That makes you tingle.
You are really flying high.
I know you enjoyed that.

Non verbal reinforcers

Being near a child
Patting
Touching a child
Hugging
Holding a child's hand
Smiling
Looking up
Winking
Raising eyebrows
Laughing
Nodding head
Clapping
Snapping fingers
Swinging arms
Hand gestures
OK signal

Thumbs up — "Fonz"

Appendix B

Interest Finder Chart

The teacher can construct a chart listing activities which can serve as reinforcers for children in her classroom. She can mark activities which each child enjoys or have children indicate their preference for a given activity. Ratings are shown in terms of high, moderate, or low interest.

Activity	**Circle Level**		
1. Easel Painting	H	M	L
2. Lotto games	H	M	L
3. Language Master	H	M	L
4. Puzzles	H	M	L
5. Crayons	H	M	L
6. Collage	H	M	L
7. Woodworking	H	M	L
8. Weaving	H	M	L
9. Filmstrip	H	M	L
10. Computer	H	M	L
11. Sitting with a friend	H	M	L
12. Lincoln Logs	H	M	L
13. Water & Sand Table	H	M	L
14. Blockbuilding	H	M	L
15. Record Player	H	M	L
16. Free Choice	H	M	L

Appendix C

Observational Analysis

The text has discussed the importance of observations which help the teacher analyze problems and probable solutions. Several anecdotal observations are included in this section. We would suggest that the student study these "samples" and construct some hypotheses concerning the participants in the observations. Students may also wish to discuss how they would change the behaviors noted in these observational vignettes.

Observation of Camp Setting

This observation was taken verbatim from a group of eight, ten year old boys in a camp setting. Note that each statement is numbered. An analysis of the interaction is presented following the observation. The Counselor (Cs) is discussing kinds of possible program activities with the group:

1. Cs: O.K., I'm ready — come over here and sit down. I'm open to suggestions.
2. Adam: Let's pack supper and go on an overnight hike.
3. Cs: H'm-m-m...
4. Bill: Let's have a nature hike.

5. Cs: That's a good idea. What do we need for a nature hike?
6. Dick: We need six-twelve for mosquitoes.
7. Adam: How about an overnight hike?
8. Cs. One at a time — what else do we need for a nature hike?
9. Peter: We could ask Joy (the nature counselor) to go with us and point out the flowers and leaves.
10. Cs. That's a good idea. That would be quite educational. What else for the nature hike?
11. Mitch: How about, Capture the Flag.
12. Cs: H'm-m-m ... Tom, aren't you going to contribute? These ideas must come from everyone.
13. Tom: Capture the Flag.
14. Cs: Somebody has already mentioned that. Now, what else do we need to take for our nature hike?
15. Dick: Take canteens, knives and hatchets.
16. Cs: Fine. Now, shall we go swimming and boating?
17. All Yeah!
18. Cs: Swimming?
    All: Yes, let's go swimming (consensus).
19. Cs: Boating?
20. Adam: How about an overnight hike?
21. Cs: We are voting for boating now. Who wants boating?
22. All: Yeah, Okay (consensus).
23. Cs: Good, that's settled. Any suggestions for outside games?
24. Bill: Let's play ball with Pedro's cabin.
25. Adam leaves the group at this point and starts for the door of the cabin.
26. Cs: Where are you going, Adam? We need everyone's help during program planning.
27. Adam: I'm going to the bathroom (leaves).

28. Cs: Okay ... well, I guess we are all set now.
Someone better go over to Pedro's cabin and
see if they want to play ball with us.
(Note: The recorder stopped at this point.)

Analysis and comment

A superficial glance would indicate that the discussion taking place was held in a democratic fashion. A quick tabulation would indicate that six of the eight children in the group made contributions to the discussion. A cursory examination also reveals (items 17 and 22) that the group voted. Items 2, 7, and 20 indicate "opportunity" for a minority opinion to be voiced. Thus, we see the elements of the democratic process in action: discussion, voting, minority and majority opinion. Unfortunately, closer examination reveals that our example of democracy never advanced beyond the surface elements.

One item that becomes apparent is the overwhelming domination of the leader during the group discussion. This can be observed in several ways: (a) The group leader made 14 of the 28 responses during the discussion. (Note: In five days of observing this group, the leader made approximately 45 percent of the responses during planning and group discussion time.) (b) Both conscious (items 8, 14, and 21) and unconscious (item 3) statements are made to the group in an effort to rebuff certain suggestions from group members. (c) From item 1 to item 16 we observe a move on the part of the leader from hearing suggestions and exploring possibilities to a final decision. Item 16 indicates the leader has made a decision without any group consensus. Items 5, 8, and 10 seem only tools which the leader manipulates in order to move the group to his own ends. (d) Of the four activities suggested (nature hike, swimming, boating, outside games) — only one idea came from the group per se.

A second unfortunate consequence is Adam. Constantly rebuffed by the leader, (Items 3, 7, 25), he finally leaves the

189

situation. Items 12 and 26 also reveal a very disturbing factor. These statements indicate a verbal acceptance of the democratic process on the part of the leader. One can conjecture that while the leader is actually forcing group decisions, he seems to be of the opinion that he is getting group decision and participation.

One final note: The results of this type of group management seem best summarized by the following incident which occurred about a week later. At breakfast two of the boys approached one of the authors and the following conversation took place:

Peter: We are going on a hot dog roast tonight.
KO: Hey, that's nice! Where will you go?
Peter: I don't know.
Adam: The counselor knows. That's all that matters.

Observation of snack period

The Head Teacher of a four year old group approached us with a problem. As she remarked: "Our snack period is very hectic. No one seems to stop or even slow down."

We observed the snack period for ten consecutive days. One of these observations is presented below. The pacing and verbal content are typical of all ten observations.

The teacher has prepared the juice table in the corner of the room. Grape juice and crackers have been placed on the table. The teacher has poured the juice from a large pitcher into two smaller ones. Some of the children have already had their juice as the observation begins:

1. T: "Everybody come and get juice."
2. Sara: "This just makes me hungrier." (Drinks juice)
3. T: "Why don't you have some more?"
4. Sara: (Pours another glass) "This just makes me hungrier. "

190

5. T: Jimmie runs near the table. T says, "Jimmie, go wash your hands and have some juice."

6.   Cashmere runs by the table, picks up a cracker and runs off.

7. T: "Everybody come and get juice."

8. T: "Sean, come have juice now."

9. Sean: "I have had it already."

10. T: "Maria, do you want a cup?"

11.   Maria does not reply verbally, but accepts juice from the teacher.

12. T: "Everybody come and get juice."

13. Carol: (Shouting) "Everybody come and get juice!" Then, in a more subdued tone, "I'm gonna take two cups." She fills two cups and spills some juice on the table. She quickly gulps down both cups and leaves the table.

14.   Teacher cleans up the juice which Carol spilled.

15. T: Tanya comes to the table. T. hands Tanya a pitcher and says, "Have some juice."

16. Amos: "I want some juice."

17. T: "Here's the pitcher."

18. Amos: "It's empty!"

19. T: Goes over to the sink and gets another small pitcher of juice. Returns to the table and gives the pitcher to Amos saying, "Here you are, more juice."

20. T: "Last call, did everyone get their juice?"

Analysis and comment

The snack period should be a time to pause and relax. It is an excellent opportunity for the teacher to talk with various children and encourage social interaction. However, in this observation one can sense the feeling of disorganization during the snack period. Notice that the overall "theme" in the teacher's verbal behavior seems to be: "Everyone come and get juice." In this report there are twelve separate items of teacher interaction. Unfortunately every item refers specifically to juice and crackers. The teacher makes no effort to positively reinforce, "sitting behavior" or social interchange.

The teacher does not make use of her children as helpers and thereby, misses an opportunity to provide a good learning experience. The children could have been used to set the table, mix the juice, place the napkins — plus other tasks. By helping the teacher, children have the opportunity to reinforce vital social and cognitive skills. Item 14 suggests that the teacher might have asked Carol to clean up. In item 19 she could have had Amos go get another pitcher of juice. Item 13 deserves special mention: In this item we see Carol model the teacher's verbal behavior.

Observation of Classroom setting

The following observation was taken in a classroom of first grade children. The children have just come in from recess. The teacher is planning to start an arithmetic lesson. Rob and Jeremy begin to fight and are told to go "stand in the hall." The class is quite noisy; children are wandering about the room and the teacher appears quite agitated.

1. T: "Everyone get in their seats and get quiet!"
2. T: (thirty seconds pass) Teacher goes over to the light switch and switches the overhead light out for several seconds. (very loud, almost shouting) "Do you know what lights out mean?" There is no noticeable change in the classroom noise level.
3. T: Switches lights on and off rapidly four times saying, "Do you know what lights out mean?"
4. Amy: "Ms. Morton, may I go get a drink of water?"
5. T: "Amy, I am trying to get this class quiet. No, you may not get a drink of water."
6. Amy walks back to the door. When the teacher is not looking, Amy scoots out the door.
7. T: "I am still waiting for quiet."
8. During this period Scott and Dante are in a scuffle over a paper clip. Scott gets it and

twists it into the shape of a gun.

9. T: (switches lights) "Do you know what lights out mean?"

10. Two children are under a table. The teacher approaches them and says, "Rob, you and Camille go stand in the hall and get quiet!" (Pause, then in a loud voice) Everybody get in your seats!"

11. Scott: "Dante isn't in his seat!"

12. T: "Okay, Scott, you told me ... get in your seat, Dante. Everybody, please close your mouth and zip it up!"

13. T: (thirty seconds pass) "Everybody freeze!"

14. Most children stop for a few seconds at this command; but the activity quickly begins to pick up again.

15. T: "You are not paying attention. I know some boys that don't know the meaning of following directions.

16. T: Goes to the light switch. Flips lights. "I am going to count to three. I am sure I can think of some extra writing for you to do."

17. T: "One ... two ... three ... extra writing for Gary, Shane, and Scott." Shane and Scott finally take their seats.

18. Amy returns to the room.

19. T: "Amy, take your seat."

20. T: Most children are now in their seats. The teacher says, "Let's all count to ten."

21. Children count to ten in unison.

22. "Gary, take your seat."

23. Rob: (from the hallway) "Ms. Morton, will you give us another chance?"

24. T: "Rob, you are going to have to stay out there and be quiet - so zip your mouth up!"

25. T: "Let's all turn to page 93 in our math book."

The observer notes: "Although most children are in their seats, few are paying attention and most of the children are still talking. Two boys crawl under a table. They are under the table for three minutes."

26. T: "Gil, get out from under the table!"
27. T: Shannon goes to the front of the room, gets some animal crackers and starts passing them out to the children.
28. T: "Shannon, I did not ask you to pass out cookies — we are doing arithmetic now!"

Analysis and comment

Obviously this teacher is experiencing some management difficulties in restoring order to the class and in making a transition to arithmetic. Analysis of this observation is being omitted to provide the reader with an opportunity to diagnose the management problems and offer some suggestions on how the teacher could improve. Hint: Analyze the teachers "open" and then count the number of positive reinforcers in this observation.

Appendix D

Ratings, Contracts and Assessment

The following items are designed to help you assess yourself and your teaching by: a) analyzing the source of your problems in maintaining discipline, and b) determining if you are meeting your goals.

Keep a "problem log"

We suggest the following procedure: At the beginning of the school day, designate a specific problem or area which you wish to record for that day's session. In some cases you may wish to keep the log on a specific problem for several days. The following problems or areas may help you to evaluate your specific shortcomings in discipline or classroom management.

a. Make a list of specific problems you encountered today. How did you handle the problems? Were you clear? consistent? firm?

b. Keep track of prohibitions which you "meted out" to students. Do you have too many rules? Are your rules too picky? Remember: The more rules you have, the more rules students break. Did you offer the students an alternative? Did you provide a cushion?

c. Make a list of specific students with whom you have difficulty in setting firm limits.

d. List your three "most difficult" students. Itemize their specific problems. Map out some strategies of ways you can help these students with their problems.

e. List two or three situations which were upsetting to you today. Try to determine the reason or reasons that these events upset you. (Hint: Re-read the section entitled, "Am I the Problem" in Chapter One.)

f. What methods did you use to communicate to students that you were dissatisfied with their performance? Were you clear and specific — did the students really understand the source of the problem?

g. Did you help children understand and accept the consequences of their actions? Did you follow through?

h. What positive reinforcers did you use? Were they effective? Were you consistent in your reinforcements?

i. Did you make contact with all of the students today? Did all the students know (through your recognition and assurance) that you were aware of their presence today and interested in their activities? Did you avoid any problem children? Did you forget to notice the "quite" child?

Examining a specific problem

Suggestion: Re-read Chapter One. Some of the material below is taken from this chapter.

a. Describe the child's problem or problems. Study the section on "Determining the Problem" in Chapter One. What specific behavior or behaviors are inappropriate? What changes need to be made in order to obtain behaviors which will be acceptable? What do you plan to do if you do not get acceptable behavior?

b. Ask yourself: Am I the problem? Is there something that I am doing which is contributing to this child's behavior?

c. Does the child have a physical problem? What is the child's learning ability? Am I expecting too much? Is there some unknown situation in the home or the school environment? Is there a developmental problem? What is the child's role in the peer group?

Student ratings of the teacher

Some teachers may wish to design a rating scale in order for children to rate the teacher's performance in certain areas. You can devise items in terms of your discipline, your general teaching skills, specific subject matter skills, as well as personality attributes.

Prior to having students do the rating, the teacher should discuss the purpose of the ratings — their advantages and shortcomings. Of course, the ratings should be anonymous if they are to be truly effective. Two typical formats and sample items are presented below.

Directions:

Below are some items for you to rate. Circle the response that most nearly presents your feelings. Remember that you do not have to place your name on the paper, so be completely honest in your evaluation.

Circle the correct response:

1) Generally my teacher is:
 Very friendly   Friendly   Not too friendly

2) Our math lesson was:
 Very interesting   So-so   Fair   Boring

3) Our homework assignments are:
 Too long   About right   Too short

Directions:

I would like to know how you feel about our Interest Centers. Would you place an "x" in the box which most nearly represents your feelings? Remember you do not have to identify yourself, so please give me your honest opinion.

Item	Excellent	Very good	Okay	Fair	Poor
Reading Center					
Math Center					
Science Center					
Art Center					

Contracts

Contracts are used in many phases of everyday life. A contract is a binding agreement between two individuals and states certain conditions which must be met. Utilizing Skinner's theory of operant conditioning, some researchers in the area of behavior modification have employed contracting. A contract should specify the precise performance standards which should be attained in order to receive the stated reward.

Contracts can be helpful in situations where students find work uninteresting and have little motivation to carry out a specific assignment. Contracting is a method for individualizing class instruction and permitting teachers to work "one-on-one" with a student by specifying specific tasks and goals. Contracts emphasize student self-control, self-management and monitoring of one's own activities. Certainly, contracting has proved helpful in getting work accomplished. The steps to take are as follows: a) Keep the contract simple. We have seen some contracts which appear to be worded by a "Philadelphia Lawyer." If the contract is simple and the goals are specific, the student can usually be responsible to monitor his own behavior. b) The teacher and pupil agree on a specific area to be covered by the contract. Studies in this area suggest the following: The contract should be jointly determined — with the student taking an active part in determining the task and the conditions of the contract. The contract should not be a unilateral document. The contract should be based on a small task and one which can be successfully completed within a relatively short period of time. c) The contract should clearly state the conditions. For example, "When ten math problems are completed correctly, the student may work with puppets, use the computer, or look at filmstrips for the remainder of the period." d) The teacher should observe the student to make sure that the contract is being fulfilled. e) It is advisable to set a "completion date" when the contract will be terminated and a new contract can be negotiated. f) Wherever possible, have students monitor their own behavior. Research has shown that when students monitor their own behavior and maintain daily records, a significant improvement in behavior occurs.

There can be problems with contracting. Sometimes there is high interest on the part of the student, but after the initial enthusiasm wears off, the old problem remains and the teacher is back where she started.

Some teachers may feel that this type of arrangement is just a technique to manipulate the student or it represents a sophisticated bribe. However, it should be pointed that most of us do sign contracts for our work. There are instances when the adult may need to provide "extrinsic rewards" until the child learns the joys of doing a particular task. When this has occurred, the child will accomplish the task for its own intrinsic reward.

Appendix E

Glossary of Drug Terms

Acapulco Gold	High grade of marijuana
Ace	Marijuana cigarettes
Acid	LSD
Acid head	Frequent user of LSD (hophead)
Angel dust	PCP
Artillery	Equipment for injections
Base	Cocaine used for freebasing
Bag, lid	Packet of drugs. (In grass: 3/4 oz.)
Bagman	Supplier of "bags" or drugs
Bennies	Amphetamine
Blow a stick	Smoke marijuana
Blow your nose	Snort cocaine
Blue devils	Amytal
Boxed	In jail
Brick	Kilogram of marijuana
Bummer (Bum trip)	Bad experience with psychedelics
Buzz	Try to buy drugs
"C"	Cocaine
Candy	Barbiturates
Cannabis	Scientific name for marijuana
Clean	Off drugs
Coke	Cocaine
Cold turkey	Off drugs, withdrawal from drugs

Cooker	Spoon or bottle cap used to heat drug for an injection
Crack	Smokable cocaine
Crank	Amphetamine
Cut	Dilute drugs by adding milk sugar
Deck	Small packet of heroin
Dime bag	$10.00 pkg. of drugs; usually pot
Dope	Heroin or other narcotics
Downers	Sedatives, depressant drug
Dynamite	Cocaine and morphine mixture
Fix	Injection of narcotics
Flea powder	Poor quality narcotics
Footballs	Oval shaped amphetamines
Freakout	Bad drug experience
Free base	Smoking cocaine
Gluey	Person who inhales glue
Good trip	Good experience with psychedelics
Grass	Marijuana (also called: Pot, grass, weed, dope, Mary Jane, MJ)
"H"	Heroin
Half load	15 decks of heroin
Hash	Hashish, resin of Cannabis
Hard stuff	Heroin
Head Shop	Store selling drug related items
Heat	Police
High	Under the influence. Also called: stoned, buzzed, fried, bombed
Hooked	Addicted
Horse	Heroin
Hype	Drug addict
Joint	Marijuana cigarette
Joy Pop	Occasional injection
Junkie	Addict
Kick the habit	Stop drug usage
Kilo	1 Kilogram or 35 ounces
Lid	One ounce of marijuana
Load	30 decks of heroin
Love-weed	Marijuana
"M"	Morphine

Mainline	Inject drug into veins
Manicure	Remove seeds, sticks from pot
Mule	Transporter of narcotics
Narco (Nark)	Narcotics officer
Nickel bag	$5.00 pkg. of drugs
O.D.	Overdose of narcotics
On ice	To be in jail
On the bricks	Out of jail
Parlay	Large piece of crack
Pee Wee	Part of a parlay
Pep pills	Amphetamines
Pusher	Drug dealer
Red Devils	Seconal
Reefer	Marijuana cigarette
Roach	Marijuana butt
Rock	Smokable cocaine
Score	Make a drug purchase
Shoot	Inject drugs
Shooting gallery	Place where addicts gather
Skag	Heroin
Skin popping	Injecting drugs under the skin
Snort	Sniffing cocaine or heroin
Snow	Cocaine
Speed	Cocaine or methamphetamine
Spoon	Sixteenth of an ounce
Steam boat	Roach holder (toilet roll)
Stoned	Under the influence of drugs
Strung out	Heavily addicted
Stuff	Any drug (usually heroin)
TCH	Main chemical in marijuana
Tea Party	Marijuana party
Toke up	To smoke marijuana
Trip	Getting high on psychedelics
Turned on	Under the influence
Weed	Marijuana
Weekend habit	Small, irregular drug habit
Yellow jacket	Nembutal

Suggested References

Anderson, L., Evertson, C., & Emmer, E. (1979). *Dimensions in classroom management derived from recent reearch.* Austin: University R & D Ctr. for Teacher Education. ERIC Document Reproduction Service No. ED 175-860.

Arlin, M. (1979). Teacher transitions can disrupt time flow in classrooms. *American Educational Research Journal,* **16**, 42-56.

Bailey, R., & Kackley, J. (1975). *Positive alternatives to school suspensions.* St. Petersburg: Personnel Services Demonstration Project.

Bandura, A. (1973). *Aggression: A social learning theory.* Englewood Cliffs, NJ: Prentice-Hall.

Bandura, A. (1986). *Social foundations of thought and action.* Englewood Cliffs, NJ: Prentice-Hall.

Becker, W. (1975). *Parents are teachers.* Champaign, IL: Research Press.

Bee, H. (1988). *The developing child.* New York: Harper & Row.

Berliner, D. (1989). Changing minds to change behavior. *Instructor,* **44**, (6), 20-21.

Brophy, J. (1979). Teacher behavior and its effects. *Journal of Educational Psychology,* **71**, 733-750.

Brophy, J. (1982). Supplemental group management techniques. In Daniel Duke, Ed., *Helping Teachers Manage Classrooms.* Washington: ASCD.

Brophy, J., & Evertson, C. (1976). *Learning from teaching: A developmental perspective.* Boston: Allyn and Bacon.

Brophy, J. & Evertson, C. (1978). Context variables in teaching. *Eucational Psychologist* , **12**, 310-316.

Caldwell, B. (1977). Agression and hostility in young children. *Young Children,* **32,** 4-13.

Canter, L. (1976). *Assertive discipline.* Los Angeles: Lee Canter & Associates.

Canter, L. (1988). Assertive discipline and the search for the perfect classroom. *Young Children,* **43,** (2), 24.

Cherry, C. (1983). *Please don't sit on the kids.* Belmont, CA: Pittman Learning.

Clewett, A. (1988). Guidance and discipline: Teaching young children appropriate behavior. *Young Children,* **43,** (4), 26-31.

Cohen, D., & Stern, V. (1958). *Observing and recording the behavior of young children.* New York: Teachers College Press.

Coloroso, B. (1983). *Discipline: Winning at teaching.* Boulder, CO: Kids, Inc.

Cryan, J. (1987). The banning of corporal punishment. *Childhood Education,* **63,** 146-153.

Diebert, A., & Harmon, A. (1971). *New tools for changing behavior.* Champaign, IL: Research Press.

Dittman, L. (1988). The mentally retarded child. In *Childcraft: Guide for Parents*, Volume 15. Chicago: World Book, Inc.

Dollard, J., & Miller, N. (1950). *Personality and Psychotherapy*. New York: MGraw-Hill.

Duke, D. , Ed. (1982). *Helping Teachers Manage Classrooms*. Washington: ASCD.

Dunaway, J. (nd) How to cut discipline problems in half. In *Discipline: Day by day*. Washington: NEA (cassette).

Dunn, R. (1983). Learning style and its relation to exceptionality at both ends of the spectrum. *Exceptional Children*, **49**, 496-506.

Dunn, R., & Dunn, K. (1978). *Teaching students through their individual learning styles*. Reston, VA: Reston.

Elardo, R., & Caldwell, B. (1973). Value imposition in early childhood. *Child Care Quarterly*, **10**, 6-13.

Emmer, E. (1988). Classroom management and discipline. In Richardson-Koehler, Ed., *Educator's handbook: A research perspective*. New York: Longman Inc.

Emmer, E., Evertson, C., & Anderson, L. (1980). Effective classroom management at the beginning of the school year. *Elementary School Journal*, **80**, 219-231.

Emmer, E., et al. (1984). *Classroom management for secondary teachers*. Englewood Cliffs: Prentice-Hall.

Epstein, C. (1980). *Classroom management and teaching*. Reston, VA: Reston.

Evertson, C., et al. (1989). *Classroom management for elementary teachers*. Englewood Cliffs: Prentice-Hall.

Fleming, R. (1973). The supervisor as an observer. In Beegle, C., & Brandt, R., Eds., *Observational methods in the classroom*. Washington: ASCD.

Gartrell, D. (1987). Assertive discipline: Unhealthy for children and other living things. *Young Children*, **42**, (2), 10-11.

Gartrell, D. (1987). Punishment or guidance? *Young Children*, **42**, (3), 55-61.

Gearheart, B., & Weishahn, M. (1976). *The handicapped child in the regular classroom*. St. Louis: C.V. Mosby

Glasser, W. (1969). *Schools without failure*. New York: Harper and Row.

Glasser, W. (1977). Ten steps to good discipline. *To-day's Education*, **66**, 61-63.

Gnagey, W. (1969). *Controlling classroom misbehavior*. Washington: NEA. (filmstrip also available)

Gump, P. (1982). School settings and their keeping. In Daniel Duke, Ed., *Helping Teachers Manage Classrooms*. Washington: ASCD.

Hansen, W. (1988). Effective school-based approaches to drug abuse prevention. *Educational Leadership*, **45**, (6), 9-14.

Hallahan, D., & Kauffman, J. (1988). *Exceptional Children*. Englewood Cliffs: Prentice-Hall.

Hetherington, M., Cox, M., & Cox, R. (1979). Play and social interaction in children following divorce. *Journal of Social Issues*, **35**, 26-49.

Hitz, R. (1988). Assertive discipline: A response to Lee Canter. *Young Children* , **43**, (2), 25-26.

Honig, A. (1985a). Compliance, control and discipline: Part I. *Young Children,* **40**, (2), 50-58.

Honig, A. (1985b). Compliance, control and discipline: Part II. *Young Children,* **40**, (3), 47-52.

Honig, A. (1986a). Stress and coping in young children: Part I. *Young Children,* **41**,(4), 50-63.

Honig, A. (1986b). Stress and coping in young children: Part II. *Young Children,* **41**, (5), 47-59.

Hoffman, M. (1970). Moral development. In Carmichael's *Manual of Child Psychology.* New York: Wiley.

Hunter, M. (1980). Altering the alterable variables. *Educational Forum,* **45**, 121-122.

Hunter, M. (1981). *Increasing your teaching effectiveness.* Palo Alto, CA: Learning Institute.

Hyman, I., & D'Alessandro, J. (1984). Good old-fashioned discipline: The politics of punitiveness. *Phi Delta Kappan,* **66**, 39-45.

Hyman, I., & Wise, J., Eds. (1979) *Corporal punishment in American education.* Philadelphia: Temple University Press.

Jackson, P. (1968). *Life in classrooms.* New York: Holt, Rinehart and Winston.

Johnson, L., et al. (1986). *Drug use among American high school students, college students, and other young adults.* Rockville, MD: NIDA.

Jones, V. (1982). Training teachers to be effective class-room managers. In Daniel Duke, Ed., *Helping Teachers Manage Classrooms.* Washington: ASCD.

Jones, V., & Jones, L. (1986). *Comprehensive Classroom Management.* (2nd Ed.). Boston: Allyn and Bacon.

Joyce, B., & Weil, M. (1980). *Models of teaching.* Engle-wood Cliffs: Prentice-Hall.

Kandall, D. (1975). Stages in adolescent involvement in drug use. *Science,* **190,** 912-914.

Kephart, N. (1974). *The slow learner in the classroom,* Columbus, OH: C.E. Merrill.

Kounin, J. (1970). *Discipline and group management in classrooms.* New York: Holt, Rinehart and Winston.

Kounin, J., & Gump, P. (1958). The ripple effect in disci-pline. *The Elementary School Journal,* **35,** 158-162.

Lewis, R., & St. John, N. (1974). Contribution of cross-racial friendship to minority group achievement. *Sociometry,* **37,** 79-91.

Lippitt, R., & White, R. (1940). The social climate of children's groups. In Barker, Kounin, & Wright, Eds. *Child behavior and development.* New York: McGraw-Hill.

Madsen, C., & Madsen, C. (1981). *Teaching/ Discipline: A positive approach for educational development.* Boston: Allyn and Bacon.

Manning, B. (1988). Application of cognitive behavior modification: First and third graders' self-management of classroom behaviors. *American Educational Research Journal,* **25,** 193-212.

Manning, B. (1989). *Cueing classroom self-control.* Unpublished manuscript. Athens, GA : University of Georgia.

Meichenbaum, D. (1977). *Cognitive behavior modification: An integrative approach.* New York: Plenum.

Mussen, P., Ed. (1983). *Handbook of child psychology.* New York: John Wiley & Sons.

NAEYC. (1988). Ideas that work with young children: Avoiding "me against you" discipline. *Young Children,* **44**, (1), 24-31.

NSSE. (1979). NSSE Yearbook. *Classroom Management.* Chicago: University of Chicago Press.

Ofchus, L. (1980). *Effects on non-target classmates of teachers' efforts to control deviant behavior.* Unpublished doctoral dissertation, Wayne State University.

Osborn, D. (1962). *Saliencies in students' perceptions of teachers.* Unpublished doctoral dissertation, Wayne State University.

Osborn, D. (1968). Permissiveness re-examined. In M. Rasmussen, Ed., *Readings in Childhood Education.* Washington: ACEI.

Purkey, W. (1978). *Inviting school success: A self-concpt aproach to teaching and learning.* Belmont, CA: Wadsworth.

Read, M. (1986). *Malnutrition, learning and behavior.* Washington: NICHD Publication No. NIH 76-1036.

Rosenthal, R., & Jacobson, L. (1968). *Pygmalion in the classroom.* New York: Holt Rinehart and Winston.

Rowen, B. (1973). *The children we see.* New York: Holt, Rinehart and Winston.

Sanford, J., Clements, B., & Emmer, E. (1983). Improving classroom management. *Educational Leadership,* **40**, 56-61.

Sears, R., Maccaoby, E., & Levin, H. (1957). *Patterns of child rearing.* Evanston: Row Peterson and Co.

Sherman, S., et al. (1983). The false consensus effect in estimates of smoking prevalence. *Personality and Social Psychology Bulletin* ,**9**, 197-207.

Sigel, I., Hoffman, M., Dreyer, A., & Torgoff, I. (1957). Influence techniques used by parents to control the behavior of children. *American Journal of Orthopsychiatry,* **27**, 356-364.

Skeen, P., & McKenry, P. (1980). The teacher's role in facilitating a child's adjustment to divorce. *Young Children,* **35,** (1), 3-12.

Soulis, M. (1988). Adolescents, alcohol, and drugs. *Independent School,* **47**, (2), 31-37.

Vygotsky, L. (1934). *Thought and Language.* Cambridge: MIT Press.

Wallen, C., & Wallen, L. (1978). *Effective Classroom Management.* Boston: Allyn and Bacon.

Author Index

Subject Index